The X-Files: Fight the Future

Jose Escobar

FADE IN:

EXT. SNOWSCAPE
A BLINDING WHITE SCREEN, under which we hear an ominous low end Dolby THX Big Screen rumble. We're not in 19" television land anymore, Toto. As the rumble builds, TWO BLACK FIGURES appear on what now has resolved into a distant horizon. From their movements we can shortly see that the figures are men. Moving along a windswept ice sheet in an otherwise featureless land.
A LEGEND appears: NORTH TEXAS, 35,000 B. C.

CLOSER ON THE TWO MEN
Continuing toward us, we can now see that they are dressed in crude garments made of animal skins. If we squint we can see their hair is long, their jutting foreheads significant of primitive Homo Sapiens. They continue toward us, the wind beating against them, CAMERA IS CRANING DOWN to the snow that lies before them. To LARGE THREE-TOED TRACKS.

FOLLOWING THE PRIMITIVES
As they track the three-toed prints to a rocky crevice in the hard-pack ice. The prints stop here, and so do the men. Dropping down into the crevice in pursuit of their quarry.

INT. ICE CAVE

Dark in here, except where the sunlight penetrates the thick, glassy ice walls. The silhouettes of the Primitives stark against the glistening cavern. The sound of flint being struck, then A TORCH CATCHES FIRE, illuminating their faces. And:

A CREATURE
Deeper in the cave. Fleeing the light and the men. We get only a brief glimpse of it in the torch light, seeing that it moves upright on two legs and has gray, dinosaur-like skin. And large black eyes. But it moves quickly enough away that any other identifying feature is lost in the deeper shadows.

THE PRIMITIVES
Removing crude weapons made of sharpened bone from under their thick fur garments, and scrabbling into the constricting cavern, giving chase.
Following them as they moves with animal-like agility through the tightening space. Predatory hunters. Their torchlight catching:

THE CREATURE
As it disappears into a tight opening in a smaller crevice leading off the main one. The Primitives entering frame after a moment, only a few steps behind.

The LEAD PRIMITIVE dropping to the cave floor, pulling himself into this same tight fissure in pursuit.
Splitting off from his partner who exits frame still on the run.

INT. SMALLER ICE CAVE - HIGH ANGLE DOWN
The fiery torch comes through first, held by the lead man. Throwing dancing shadows on the walls of what appears to be a box cavern.

CLOSE ON LEAD PRIMITIVE
Rising quickly to his feet. Not seeing what the torch illuminates just behind him: The face of a dead Primitive Man, his body frozen into the ice. He does finally notice this, turning to see it, when he's

ATTACKED VICIOUSLY FROM BEHIND.
The torch falls to the floor so that the fight is difficult to see, but it is loud and cruel. The creature squealing wildly as the grunts of the Primitive now turn to the sounds of painful struggle. Until:

THE SECOND PRIMITIVE MAN
Suddenly appears, driving his bone weapon into the body of the Creature. Again and again, until the Creature is driven away into the shadows.
The Second Man grabs the torch now, not to see if his hunting mate has survived, but in pursuit of the Creature. In the light we see that he and his weapon are covered with spatters of OILY BLACK BLOOD. As is the First Primitive whose body lies heaving on the floor.
The Second Primitive stepping over his hunting mate, stalking the Creature into the shadows, where it has collapsed. The torch finally landing, for the first time, on its face.
When the torchlight hits its face, the Creature attacks.
But the Primitive prevails. He drops his torch and dispatches the already wounded Creature with strong hard stabs of his weapon, one of which penetrates the
Creature's eye.

LOW ANGLE ON THE DEAD CREATURE
The torch, which lies on the ground, illuminates the dead creature's face. Its wounds are flowing with the oily black blood, which, oddly now, BEGINS TO POOL. As if it has intelligence, sentience. Pooling and traveling into a fissure in the cave floor. And disappearing.

ANGLE ON THE SECOND PRIMITIVE
Watching this, unknowing. His chest heaving from the fight, as the spots of Oily Black Blood which have spattered onto him begin to crawl. Crawling toward his eyes and mouth. Causing him to let out grunts of fear.
Which are the sounds we hear as the CAMERA SLOWLY CRANES

UP past the struggling Primitive to the roof of the cave, where the dancing shadows of the torch FADE AWAY with the sounds of struggle. Moving into darkness and silence. But only for a moment. Until:

SUNSHINE BREAKS THROUGH THE ROOF OF THE CAVE - PRESENT DAY
Along with the spade of a shovel. And then -- the earthen cave ceiling gives way and A BOY wearing Nikes and an old t-shirt falls through it. Falling PAST CAMERA. We hear a YELL, then a THUD, and a CLATTERING of the shovel that's fallen in with him. Then a pained

GASPING.
Then SEVERAL HEADS appear in the opening. These are BOYS of ten to eleven, staring down into the cave. Hot sunlight blazing in. We have traveled far, far forward in time.

2ND BOY
Hey, Stevie. You okay?

INT. CAVE - PRESENT DAY
THEIR POV OF STEVIE
On the floor below covered with dirt, in his nose and mouth. Spitting out. (All these boys have Texas in their voices.)

STEVIE
I got... I got... . I got... .
(straining)
... . the wind knocked out of me.
This draws no sympathy from above, only LAUGHTER.

THE BOYS UP ABOVE
Staring excitedly.

3RD BOY
Looks like a cave or something.

2ND BOY
What's down there, Stevie? Anything?

OVER THE BOYS ABOVE
Stevie has gotten up, moving out of the patch of sunlight. Disappearing from view for a moment. Then reappearing, still spitting out dirt. But holding:

STEVIE
Human skull.
One side partially missing from the cranium. But it brings WHOOPS of delight from the boys above.

3RD BOY
Toss it up here, dude.

STEVIE
No way, buttwipe. I found it. It's mine.

ANGLE UP ON STEVIE
The other boys looking down at him. Stevie looking at the skull. Strangely, the light shines through it. It is milky, opaque, as if it's bone that's turned somehow glassy in places. Then:

STEVIE
Anyways, there's bones all over the place down here.
Stevie looks down at his feet. CAMERA FOLLOWING HIS LOOK DOWN to where there are indeed more human bones. And something else. He takes a couple of steps in place, standing in a familiar BLACK, OILY substance -- which is climbing up his tennis shoe from the rock floor, over the edge of the shoe and down into the shoe itself. Then the SKULL drops in the frame, clattering on the hard floor of the cave.

CAMERA SLOWLY RISING UP FROM STEVIE'S SHOES
Following SUBCUTANEOUS WORMS which have begun locomoting aggressively up his legs. As his whole body is WRACKED by a shivering seizure of some kind.
CAMERA RISES, following the path of the worms as they move up the legs of his shorts. Some appearing on his bare arms, but the great majority continuing up to
Stevie's neck, toward his face. Stevie stands paralyzed.
Letting out guttural sounds not dissimilar to when the wind was knocked out of him.

3RD BOY (O. S.)
Hey, Stevie... .
But Stevie cannot answer him. CAMERA CONTINUING UP to the boys above. Looking down at their friend. Their eyes go wide.

2ND BOY
You okay?
But what they see next answers that question for them.

THEIR POV OF STEVIE
His face suddenly alive with the subcutaneous worms.

Moving toward his eyes which begin filling with BLACK
OIL. Looking much now like ALIEN EYES.

CLOSE ON THE BOYS ABOVE
Freaked by what they see. And doing what any kid would do now.

3RD BOY
Hey, man. Let's get outta here.
And they do. Bolting from the hole in the top of the cave. CAMERA PUSHING UP THROUGH THIS HOLE to REVEAL we are:

EXT. SMALL DIRT FIELD - NORTHERN TEXAS - DAY
In a dirt hole that was being dug by the three kids.
RISING UP out of the hole to REVEAL the parched dirt patch where THREE KIDS are running away from us, as fast as their feet will take them. Toward A NEW HOUSING TRACT
(five floorplans to choose from, including the model home.) Disappearing into the neighborhood. A LEGEND appears: NORTH TEXAS, 1998.
CAMERA CONTINUES RISING ABOVE THE ROOFTOPS to see the surrounding expanse of empty Texas flatland. And in the distance, the DALLAS SKYLINE.
As CAMERA SETTLES, there are a few moments of nothing but the sound of the wind gently whistling across the landscape. In which we bury a short TIME CUT.

EXT. NEIGHBORHOOD - NORTHERN TEXAS - DAY
Then we HEAR it, before we see it: FIRE ENGINES pulling into the neighborhood, sirens WAILING. CAMERA DROPPING
AGAIN as the lead engine pulls up. FIREMEN are hopping off, moving to the hole the boys dug.

LOW ANGLE UP FROM BELOW GROUND LEVEL, IN THE DUGOUT HOLE
TWO firemen carrying a ladder clamber down PAST CAMERA,
THREE OTHERS appearing on their heels. The other two firemen clamber down, too.
THE CAPTAIN at the edge of the hole watching them. Holding a radio.

FIRE CAPTAIN
This is Captain Miles Cooles... we've got a rescue situation in progress...

INT. CAVE - CONTINUOUS
As the LEAD FIREMAN steps down the ladder into the cave.
He scans the darkness, illuminated only by the shaft of light permitted by the hole above. As the 2ND FIREMAN drops down next to him. The both stand motionless now, as if sensing something.

THEIR POV
Stevie's feet are just visible on the floor of the cave, a short distance away.

RESUME FIREMEN - LOW ANGLE
They start cautiously toward Stevie. CAMERA FINDING their feet. Tracking through the same OILY, BLACK
SUBSTANCE we saw bleeding from the creature thirty five thousand years ago. As they move into the shadows, we
HOLD ON THE SUBSTANCE.... and see it MOVE. It's alive.

EXT. DIRT FIELD - SHORT TIME LATER
CAMERA RISES out of the dirt hole, finds A GROUP OF

NEIGHBORS:
Concerned PARENTS, KIDS, including Stevie's friends.
They're held at a distance by the remaining firemen.
Everyone turning their concerned gazes skyward. Looking at:

A MED-EVAC CHOPPER
Coming off the sun-setting horizon. Moving toward us at high speed. The WHOP, WHOP of its blade soon shaking the neighborhood as it banks in and around and hovers just over the dirt field. Landing gently on the parched hard scrabble.
The side door flies open and FIVE HAZ-MAT RESCUE
PARAMEDICS jump out carrying a bubble litter. CAMERA
PANS THEM to the dirt hole past THE FIRE CAPTAIN. The
Haz-Mat Paramedics moving down into the hole. The Fire
Captain watches this, then stares toward --
DR. BEN BRONSCHWEIG (in shirtsleeves, tie), exiting the chopper, following up the rear. The Captain meeting him in route.

BRONSCHWEIG
(over the chopper)
Keep those people back. Get them out of here.

FIRE CAPTAIN
(to his men)
Move them all back.
(dogging Bronschweig)
I sent four men down after the boy.
They're not responding.
Dr. Bronschweig's focus is elsewhere, though. He's making a bee line to the earthen hole where young Stevie is being pulled out and lifted into an enclosed

QUARANTINE BUBBLE LITTER by the rescue squad.
Bronschweig watches with great concern. Getting a good look now at Stevie's paralyzed body as it passes him.

ANGLE ON CHOPPER
As Stevie's body is loaded aboard, the side door is slid shut. The engine throttles up and the chopper takes flight again, almost as quickly as it arrived. The prop wash blowing:

DR. BRONSCHWEIG
And the gathering crowd. Bronschweig watches the chopper bank away, then turns his look to:

THE NEIGHBORHOOD
Where A SERIES OF UNMARKED CARGO VANS, TRUCKS are rolling in. A fleet of vehicles, driven by what looks like MILITARY PERSONNEL. Most conspicuously TWO WHITE
UNMARKED TANKER TRUCKS. (There are NO MARKINGS on these vehicles.)

RESUME BRONSCHWEIG
As the Fire Captain moves around to face him off.

FIRE CAPTAIN
What about my men?

DR. BRONSCHWEIG
(brusquely)
We're doing all we can.
And he moves off toward the approaching trucks where the
MILITARY PERSONNEL are pulling out tents, tent poles, scientific equipment. Leaving the Captain to wonder what the hell's going on. Watching the first of many
REFRIGERATION UNITS being unloaded. The personnel carrying it paying him no mind as they blow past him.
Moving RIGHT TO CAMERA and plunging us into BLACK.
HOLD. Then OVER BLACK, a familiar sound again. The sound of a chopper auguring in. As we FADE UP, revealing we are:

EXT. TOP OF A SKYSCRAPER - DAY
The chopper is banking over the side of the building, preparing to touch down on the rooftop where FIFTEEN FBI
AGENTS in dark ID windbreakers are standing. A LEGEND appears: FEDERAL BUILDING, DALLAS, TEXAS. ONE WEEK

LATER.

The chopper touches down and, again, the side door is thrown open. But now only one man exits: SPECIAL AGENT

IN CHARGE (S. A. C.) DARIUS MICHAUD.
Michaud moves with the measured pace of authority, approaching the waiting FBI Agents. One of whom steps up.

FBI AGENT
We've evacuated the building and been through it bottom to top. No trace of an explosive device or anything resembling one.

S. A. C. MICHAUD
Have you taken the dogs through?

FBI AGENT
Yes, sir.

S. A. C. MICHAUD
Well, take them through again.
This is given as a non-negotiable order, to the somewhat weary FBI man. Who turns back to his charges, Michaud does not register this attitude, though. Something else has caught his attention. Causing him to walk to the edge of the building. CAMERA FOLLOWING HIM, seeing what he sees now.
On an adjacent skyscraper is what appears to be AN FBI
AGENT in an ID windbreaker exiting onto the roof. CAMERA
CONTINUING AROUND into A CLOSE UP PROFILE of S. A. C
Michaud. Staring at this, his jaw set. He doesn't like what he sees. And what he sees is:

EXT. ROOFTOP OPPOSING SKYSCRAPER - DAY - CONTINUOUS
Special Agent Dana Scully is coming out the door leading onto the roof. The door slams shut behind her. She, too, is dressed in an FBI windbreaker. She's dialing her cell phone as she moves around the rooftop looking for something. Dialing the number of:

SCULLY
Mulder -- it's me --

MULDER (FILTER)
Where are you, Scully?

SCULLY
I'm on the roof.

MULDER (FILTER)

Did you find something?

SCULLY
(impatiently)
No. I haven't.

MULDER (FILTER)
What's wrong, Scully?

SCULLY
I've just climbed twelve floors. I'm hot and thirsty and I'm wondering, to be honest, what I'm doing here.

MULDER (FILTER)
You're looking for a bomb.

SCULLY
I know that. But the threat was called in for the Federal Building across the street.

MULDER (FILTER)
I think they have that covered.

WE ARE TRACKING WITH SCULLY.
SCULLY
(impatience)
Mulder... when a terrorist bomb threat is called in, the logical purpose of providing this information is to allow us to find the bomb. The rational object of terrorism is to promote terror. If you'd study model behavioral pattern in virtually every case where a threat has turned up an explosive device. If we don't act in accordance with that data -- if you ignore it as we have done -- the chances are great that if here actually is a bomb we might not find it. Lives could be lost --
Scully, engrossed in her own argument, realizes she's been the only one speaking for the last short while. She stops walking.

SCULLY
Mulder... ?

MULDER
What happened to playing a hunch?
Scully almost JUMPS out of her own skin. The voice has come not over the phone, but from two feet away where:

ANGLE TO INCLUDE AGENT MULDER

Standing in the shadow of a large air conditioning unit.
Cracking a trademark sunflower seed between his teeth.
Clicking his cell phone off. Moving out.

SCULLY
Jesus, Mulder...

MULDER
The element of surprise, Scully.
Random acts of unpredictability. If we fail to anticipate the unforeseen or expect the unexpected in a universe of infinite possibilities, we find ourselves at the mercy of anyone or anything that cannot be programmed, categorized or easily referenced...
Mulder has moved to the edge of the building where he sails his sunflower seeds into the air. Dusting his hands off as if lost in a wistful through for just a moment.

MULDER
What are we doing up here? It's hotter than hell.
And he's on the move. Scully moving to catch up.

NEW ANGLE
Mulder is moving toward the stairs, Scully catching him.
Mulder allowing her to lead him up the steps.

SCULLY
I know you're bored in this assignment, but unconventional thinking is only going to get you into trouble now.

MULDER
How's that?

SCULLY
You've got to quit looking for what isn't there. They've closed the
X-Files. There's procedure to be followed here. Protocol.

MULDER
What do you say we call in a bomb threat for Houston. I think it's free beer night at the Astrodome.
Scully gives him a look. It's no use. She reaches the door first, grabs the knob but... it won't open. Turning to Mulder.

SCULLY
Now what?

MULDER
(suddenly nervous)
It's locked?
She wiggles the knob again.

SCULLY
So much for anticipating the unforeseen...
Scully squints into the sun, staring at Mulder. But he's quick on the draw, and realizes what she's up to. He grabs for the door and... it opens. Looking to Scully whose hard look of mock-scolding has become a smirking smile.

SCULLY
Had you.

MULDER
No you didn't.

SCULLY
Oh yeah. Had you big time.
And that's how it continues as they re-enter the stairwell, the door slamming shut behind them.

INT. BUILDING LOBBY - DAY
As an elevator DINGS and the doors open. Scully and
Mulder exit into the lobby where people move in and out.
Heads turn due to their FBI jackets. (Included atmosphere: a GROUP OF KIDS on a field trip, being led into an elevator by THEIR TEACHER.)

SCULLY
I saw your face, Mulder. There was a moment of panic.

MULDER
Panic? Have you ever seen me panic,
Scully?

SCULLY
I just did. You're buying.
Mulder fishes for change, but more out of sportsmanship.

MULDER
Alright... what'll it be: Coke, Pepsi?
A saline IV?

SCULLY
Something sweet.
Scully flashes a thin victory smile, as Mulder heads off.

INT. HALLWAY OUTSIDE VENDING MACHINE ROOM - CONTINUOUS
Mulder moving to a door with a small shingle above it which says SNACKS/BEVERAGES. As he approaches, sorting through the change he's fished up, the door opens and A
MAN IN A VENDOR'S UNIFORM appears. He makes casual and ever-so-brief eye contact with Mulder as he brushes past him. Mulder making no note of this as he moves to catch the door before it closes.

INT. SNACK AREA AND SODA VENDING MACHINE ROOM - DAY
Mulder takes a few steps down into the windowless room.
Moving past the snack machines to a LIGHTED soda machine.
Finding the correct change and plunking it in. Hitting a button, but... nothing comes out.

MULDER
Oh, come on.
He beats his fist a couple of times on the front of the machine.
Nothing. He finds more change. Plunking it in. Hits the button. Nothing. He stares at the machine a minute, then
BEATS IT HARD with his fist. Nothing.
Moving around to the back of the machine, looking for:

ANGLE ACROSS BACK OF MACHINE
Mulder's face peering in on the slim space between the machine and the wall. Reaching down and lifting the PLUG on the end of the electrical cord. It isn't plugged in.
Realizing now why the machine hasn't spit out his sodas.

RESUME FRONT ANGLE ON MACHINE
As Mulder appears, stepping very lightly in front of the machine that he was just pounding away on. Looking at it, then moving quickly to the door he entered through. Grasping the knob, but finding it... LOCKED. He jiggles the knob, pulls on it. But there's no two ways about it, he's locked in.

INT. BUILDING LOBBY - DAY
Scully stands looking at her watch. Wondering where
Mulder is. When her CELL PHONE starts ringing. She answers it.

SCULLY
Scully...

MULDER (FILTER)
Scully, I found the bomb.

SCULLY
(thinks he's joking)
Where are you, Mulder?

MULDER (FILTER)
I'm in the vending room.
Scully is on the move, but she doesn't believe him for a second.

INT. HALLWAY OUTSIDE VENDING MACHINE ROOM - CONTINUOUS
Scully appears, heard A POUNDING. Following this noise to the door Mulder is obviously on the other side of.
Tries the door.

SCULLY
Is that you pounding?

INT. SNACK AND SODA VENDING MACHINE ROOM - DAY
Mulder holds his phone to his ear, using his other hand to pound.

MULDER
Scully, get somebody to open this door.

SCULLY (FILTER)
Nice try, Mulder.
CAMERA FOLLOWING MULDER as he steps back, revealing now that he's gotten the hinged front of the coke machine open. But we can't yet see what's inside.

MULDER
Scully -- listen to me. It's in the coke machine. You've got about fourteen minutes to get this building evacuated.

INT. HALLWAY OUTSIDE VENDING MACHINE ROOM - CONTINUOUS
Scully is shaking her head. Tries the door again.

SCULLY
C'mon. Open the door.
His response to this is MORE HARD POUNDING.

SCULLY
Mulder? Tell me this is a joke.

MULDER (FILTER)
Thirteen fifty nine, thirteen fifty eight, thirteen fifty seven...
As he is doing this, Scully is bending to see:

THE KEYHOLE
It's been freshly soldered over.

INT. SNACK AND SODA VENDING MACHINE ROOM - DAY
Mulder stands pacing in front of:

AN ELABORATELY ENGINEERED EXPLOSIVE DEVICE
Wired with circuit boards, electric belts and generally looking like it would take an expert a good long time to figure out where to even start. A lot longer than the 13:58 that reads on the digital read-out.

MULDER
... thirteen fifty six...

SCULLY (FILTER)
Hang on. I'm gonna get you out of there.
The line goes dead. And off Mulder's deepening anxiety, we:

INT. BUILDING LOBBY - DAY
Scully enters like General Patton, taking charge.
Barking at the security guards who sit behind their security console.

SCULLY
I need this building evacuated and cleared out in ten minutes! I need you to get on the phone and tell the fire department to block off the city center in one mile radius around the building --

SECURITY GUARD
In ten minutes... . . ?!

SCULLY
DON'T THINK! JUST PICK UP THE PHONE
AND MAKE IT HAPPEN!
And she's moving, dialing her cell phone now.

SCULLY
(into phone)

This is Special Agent Dana Scully. I need to speak to S. A. C. Michaud. He's got the wrong building --

EXT. BUILDING - DAY
UNMARKED FBI VANS, CARS are pulling up out front.
Agents in windbreakers are exiting, moving at a run to the building. Among them S. A. C. Darius Michaud. Moving to:

ANGLE ON SCULLY
Exiting the building. Behind her, WORKERS are beginning to stream out of the building, as well as the young
FIELD TRIPPERS. Michaud meeting up with Scully mid-plaza. As the windbreaker Agents move past them, entering the building.

S. A. C. MICHAUD
Where is it?
MOVING WITH THEM now, back toward the building. As FIRE
TRUCKS are pulling up out in the street out front.
Suddenly this has the distinct feel of a situation veering out of control.

SCULLY
Mulder found it in a vending machine.
He's locked in with it.

INT. SNACK AND VENDING MACHINE ROOM - DAY
THE DIGITAL READ OUT hits 7:00. Pull back to REVEAL
MULDER staring at it. If he wasn't sweating enough on the roof, he's certainly sweating now. When his cell phone RINGS. Answering it.

MULDER
Scully?

SCULLY (FILTER)
Mulder. Move away from the door. We're coming through it.
No sooner is this said than the CAMERA WHIPS OFF MULDER to the door, where A GAS PLASMA TORCH FLAME is sizzling along the hinges.

INT. HALLWAY OUTSIDE VENDING MACHINE ROOM - CONTINUOUS
Where Michaud himself, wearing a Kevlar vest now, is wielding the torch. Expertly cutting the metal while
Scully and TWO AGENTS and TWO DALLAS BOMB SQUAD men look on. In the b. g. BUILDING EMPLOYEES are streaming out.
Michaud finishes and shuts off the torch. Yelling:

S. A. C. MICHAUD
Go.

The other Agents kick the metal door in sending it crashing to the floor. Mulder stands on the other side.

Watching Michaud pick up a heft tool kit, stepping over the downed door.

Scully right behind him. Along with the Agents, Bomb techs.

ANGLE OVER MULDER AND THE SODA MACHINE/BOMB
As Michaud steps in next to him, sizing up the time on the ticking digital readout: 4:07. And just exactly what kind of defusing work he's got cut out for him.

MULDER
Tell me this is just soda pop in those canisters.

S. A. C. MICHAUD
No. It's what it looks like. A big
I. E. D. - ten gallons of astrolite.
(studying the bomb)
Okay, get everybody out of here and clear the building.

MULDER
Somebody's got to stay with you --

S. A. C. MICHAUD
I gave you an order. Now get the hell out of here and evacuate the area.

SCULLY
Can you defuse it?

Setting his tool kit down, opening it. As the other Agents heed his word, exiting the room.

S. A. C. MICHAUD
I think so.

MULDER
You've got about four minutes to find out if you're wrong.

Michaud turns on him with unexpected intensity.

S. A. C. MICHAUD
Did you hear what I said?

SCULLY

Let's go, Mulder.
Scully starts out. Mulder stares at Michaud for a moment, but Michaud's focus is on the bomb now. He won't meet Mulder's look. Finally Mulder moves off, following Scully.
CAMERA HOLDS ON MICHAUD, just staring at the bomb. Just staring.

EXT. PLAZA OUTSIDE BOMB BUILDING - DAY - CONTINUOUS
The last of the building occupants are being hauled off in CITY BUSES which have moved in curbside. As these buses pull away, so do the fire trucks that have positioned themselves out front. And the police squad cars. As Mulder and Scully exit the front door. Moving quickly, until Mulder hits mid-plaza and slows. Scully not realizing this for a few steps, then turning.

SCULLY
What are you doing?
(off his non-response)
Mulder --
One last windbreakered Agent is exiting. Moving past them to the last cop car other than the car waiting for
Mulder and Scully.

LAST AGENT OUT
All clear.
Mulder has stopped and is looking back to the building now as Scully hustles back the few steps separating them.

MULDER
Something's wrong.

ANGLE OVER THEM TO THE WAITING CAR
As the Last Agent Out's car zooms away. Leaving only their car and the man driving it: a WINDBREAKERED

AGENT.
WINDBREAKERED AGENT
What's he doing?
The plaza is desolate now, void of life.

MULDER
Something's not right...

SCULLY
-- Mulder! Get in the car!

Scully is pulling him now. Pulling him toward the car and the obviously impatient Windbreakered Agent.

SCULLY
There's no time!

INT. SNACK AND SODA VENDING MACHINE ROOM - DAY
CLOSE ON BOMB. The seconds ticking off now, as it passes the :30 mark. CAMERA PULLING BACK, ADJUSTING to Michaud.
His tool chest is closed up, and he is sitting on it improbably. Still staring at the bomb, then pulling his head down in what appears to be resignation. As the seconds tick away.

CUT BACK TO:
EXT. PLAZA OUTSIDE BOMB BUILDING - DAY - CONTINUOUS
Mulder has relented now, against his better instincts.
Moving with Scully to the car, faster as they go. The
Windbreaker Agent standing in the open door of the driver's side. Getting in behind the wheel...

CUT BACK TO:
INT. VENDING MACHINE ROOM - CONTINUOUS
S. A. C. MICHAUD
Sitting motionless in front of the bomb as the seconds tick down. 8-7-6-5-4-3-2-1- --

HARD CUT BACK
TO:
EXT. PLAZA OUTSIDE BOMB BUILDING - DAY - CONTINUOUS
Mulder and Scully getting in the car. TRACKING BACKWARDS with them now as the Agent driving pulls away, getting only thirty, maybe forty yards when: the BOMB DETONATES and the building EXPLODES. And this is no fatwa symbolic little terror strike. This is Oklahoma City. Or do we say, Independence Day.

REVERSE ANGLE ON CAR
As all the windows blow out and the car is lifted up, slamming into the corner of a parked car. The air so quickly full of debris that it would seem the whole city has been destroyed.

RESUME BUILDING
As the debris starts to clear somewhat, much of it still floating to the ground, though. We see the fires raging on every floor. That most of the front of the building has been torn away and we can see right into many floors.

RESUME ANGLE ON CAR

Where it sits half cocked against a parked car. The air is full of debris, particulated matter. The rear door of the squad car opens now and Mulder gets out, covered with glass. Moving to the front passenger door, opening it for Scully.

MULDER
(with darkest irony)
Next time you're buying.

EXT. AERIAL SHOT OF WASHINGTON D. C. - DAY
HIGH ABOVE the U. S. capital, the entire beltway. With a LEGEND, to establish.

LOWER AND TIGHTER NOW
On the J. Edgar Hoover Building, FBI Headquarters.
Descending low on the three-sided monolith and its large interior courtyard. As another LEGEND appears, under:

WOMAN'S VOICE (V. O.)
In light of Waco, and Ruby Ridge...

INT. FBI OFFICE OF PROFESSIONAL REVIEW - DAY
A formal hearing. Several ASSISTANT DIRECTORS sit at a head table, going over documents. NAME PLACECARDS in front of them.
PANNING the group, the sound of papers shuffling, the occasional clearing of a throat creating a stale air of importance, under:

WOMAN'S VOICE (V. O.)
... there is a heightened need at the
Attorney General's office to place responsibility as early as possible.

CAMERA LANDING ON ASSISTANT DIRECTOR JANA CASSIDY
A no-nonsense 40 year-old lawyer cum FBI Agent.

CASSIDY
... for the catastrophic destruction of public property and the loss of life due to terrorist activities...
Next to Cassidy is Assistant Director WALTER SKINNER,
Mulder and Scully's former superior on the X-Files.
Looking ruefully at:

AGENT SCULLY
At a small table, the chair next to her conspicuously empty.

CASSIDY
Many details are still unclear; some agents' reports have not been filed, or have come in sketchy, without a satisfactory accounting of the events that led to the destruction in Dallas.
But we're under some pressure to give an accurate picture of what happened to the Attorney General, so she can issue a public statement.
The door to the room opens behind Scully now, and Mulder enters, his manner that of a man who knows he's late to a function.

RESUME A. D. CASSIDY
She looks up at Mulder and Scully with a stern glare.

CASSIDY
We now know that five people died in the explosion. Special Agent in Charge
Darius Michaud who was trying to defuse the bomb that had been hidden in a vending machine. Three firemen from Dallas, and a young boy.

OVER MULDER AND SCULLY
Mulder pulls out his chair to sit down, but remains standing. They trade a look. This is new news to them.

MULDER
Excuse me -- the firemen and the boy
-- they were in the building?

CASSIDY
Agent Mulder, since you weren't able to be on time for this hearing, I'm going to ask you to step outside so that we can get Agent Scully's version of the facts. So that she won't have to be paid the same disrespect.

MULDER
We were told the building was clear.

CASSIDY
You'll get your turn, Agent Mulder.
Please step out.
Mulder trades looks with:

A. D. SKINNER
Who stares at him evenly, but not unsympathetically.
He's been here with Mulder on many occasions. Seen
Mulder run up against the Bureau and its stiff conventions. Always in the middle.

MULDER
It does say there in your paperwork that we were the ones who found the bomb...

CASSIDY
Thank you, Agent Mulder. We'll call you in shortly.

RESUME MULDER, SCULLY
As Mulder slides his chair in. Scully watching him exit.

INT. HALLWAY OUTSIDE OPR HEARING ROOM - DAY
Mulder sits by himself in a chair, head down. When the door to the hearing room opens. Mulder rising as A. D. Skinner exits.

SKINNER
Sit down, they're still talking to
Agent Scully.

MULDER
About what?

SKINNER
-- They're asking her for a narrative.
They want to know why she was in the wrong building.

MULDER
She was with me.
Skinner studies Mulder, shaking his head.

SKINNER
You don't see what's going on here, do you?
(off Mulder's look)
There's four hundred million dollars in damage to the city of Dallas. Lives have been lost. No suspects have been named. So the story being shaped is this could have been prevented. That the FBI didn't do its job.

MULDER
And they want to blame us?

SKINNER
Agent Mulder -- we both know that if you and Agent Scully hadn't taken the initiative to search the adjacent building, you could have multiplied the fatalities by a hundred --

MULDER
(grasping the irony)
But it's not the lives we saved. It's the lives we didn't.

SKINNER
(reciting the dictum)
-- if it looks bad, it's bad for the

FBI --
MULDER
-- if they want someone to blame, they can blame me. Agent Scully doesn't deserve this.

SKINNER
She's in there right now saying the same thing about you.

MULDER
I breached protocol. I broke contact with the S. A. C. I ignored a primary tactical rule and left him alone with the device.

SKINNER
Agent Scully says it was she who ordered you out of the building. That you wanted to go back.
Mulder doesn't get to respond, because the door opens again and Agent Scully exits. She looks like she's been through it.

SCULLY
(to Skinner)
They're asking for you, Sir.
Skinner gives one last look to Mulder, then re-enters.
Leaving Mulder and Scully alone. Scully wearing a pained look.

MULDER
Whatever you told them in there, you don't have to protect me.

SCULLY
All I told them was the truth.

MULDER
They're trying to divide us on this,
Scully. We can't let them.

SCULLY
They have divided us, Mulder. They're splitting us up.

MULDER
(beat)
What? What are you talking about?

SCULLY
I meet with the OPR day after tomorrow for remediation and reassignment...

MULDER
Why?

SCULLY
I think you must have an idea. They cited a history of problems relating back to 1993.

MULDER
They were the ones that put us together.

SCULLY
Because they wanted me to invalidate your work, your investigations into the paranormal. But I think this goes deeper than that.

MULDER
This isn't about you, Scully. They're doing this to me.

SCULLY
They're not doing this, Mulder.
(off his look)
I left behind a career in medicine because I thought I might make a difference at the FBI. When they recruited me they told me women made up nine percent of the bureau. I felt this was not an impediment, but an opportunity to distinguish myself. But it hasn't turned out that way. And now, if I were to be transferred to
Omaha, or Wichita or some field office where I'm sure I could rise, it just doesn't hold the interest for me it once did. Not after what I've seen and done.

MULDER
You're... quitting?

SCULLY
There's really no reason left for me to stay anymore.
(off his look)
Maybe you should ask yourself if your heart's still in it, too.
The door opens to the hearing room again now. A. D.
Skinner steps part way out, gesturing to him.

SKINNER
Agent Mulder. You're up.

SCULLY
(regretfully)
I'm sorry. Good luck.
Mulder rises. Scully studying his poorly disguised hurt.
Before he turns and goes into the room.
Scully watching the door close behind him. Her feelings poorly disguised, too.

INT. DOWNSCALE D. C. BAR - NIGHT
CLOSE ON A SHOOTER OF TEQUILA being poured. CAMERA ADJUSTING to reveal the ATTRACTIVE BARMAID tipping the bottle. Pushing it across the bar to where TWO EMPTY
SHOOTERS sit, making the exchange.

BARMAID
I'd say this about exceeds your minimum daily requirement.
The person she's talking to us:

MULDER
He sits by himself on a stool, staring down at the bar.
Staring at the shooter which he spins with his fingers.

BARMAID
Gotta train for this kind of heavy lifting.
Mulder tosses back the shooter anyway. She watches him as she retrieves the small shot glass, intrigued by his dark silence.

BARMAID
Poopy day?

MULDER
Yup.

BARMAID
A woman?
(Mulder shakes his head no)
Work.
Mulder nods, pointing to the tequila bottle again. The
Barmaid agrees to pour another one, reluctantly.

ANGLE OVER TO A MAN AT THE END OF THE BAR
Staring at Mulder intently. He's older than Mulder, dressed in an old Brooke Brothers light summer suit.
Mulder notices him, feels his gaze, but doesn't give it thought.

RESUME BARMAID, MULDER
BARMAID
What do you do?

MULDER
What do I do.
(off her curious look)
I'm a key figure in an ongoing government charade. An annoyance to my superiors. A joke among my peers.
"Spooky," they call me. Spooky Mulder.
Whose sister was abducted by aliens when he was a kid. Who now chases little green men with a badge and a gun, shouting to the heavens and anyone who'll listen that the fix is in. That our government's hip to the truth and a part of the conspiracy.
That the sky is falling and when it hits it's gonna be the shitstorm of all time.
She stares at him for a moment, startled by his drunken screed. She pulls back the shooter she's just poured
Mulder.

BARMAID
I think that about does it, Spooky.

MULDER
Does what?

BARMAID
Why don't you go home to the old lady

--
MULDER
Sorry. Don't have one.
Mulder slides off his stool, noticing:

MULDER'S POV
The Watchful Man is gone.

RESUME MULDER
He feints toward the door, then reverses direction.
Heads to the back of the place.

INT. REAR OF DOWNSCALE BAR - NIGHT - CONTINUOUS
Mulder appears, moving to the bathroom door. Only to find an OUT OF ORDER sign on it. He moves to the woman's room, but it's locked. Gathering what's left of his wits, Mulder does what any red-blooded man would do in this situation. He goes to the back door of the bar and exits into the alley.

EXT. ALLEY BEHIND BAR - NIGHT
Mulder has found a place against a wall, between two dumpsters. Jerking around in surprise at the sound of a

VOICE.
WATCHFUL MAN'S VOICE
That official FBI business?

MULDER
(startled)
What?

ANGLE TO INCLUDE THE MAN FROM THE BAR
He's not far from Mulder. His name is KURTZWEIL.

KURTZWEIL
Bet the Bureau's accusing you of the same thing in Dallas.
Mulder's weirded out as the stranger moves to him un- threateningly.

MULDER
How's that?

KURTZWEIL
Standing around holding your yank while bombs are exploding.
Kurtzweil enjoys a little laugh over this.

MULDER
Do I know you?

KURTZWEIL
No. I've been watching your career for a good while. Back when you were just a promising young agent -- before that.
Mulder stares at this man as he finishes, zipping up.

MULDER
You follow me out here for a reason?

KURTZWEIL
Yeah, I did.
Kurtzweil unzips his own pants now. There is a moment; one of those awkward moments where Mulder's not sure what's about to happen. But Kurtzweil's just relieving himself, too. Shuffling up to the wall, Mulder takes this as an opportunity to head back toward the bar. But
Kurtzweil hails him again.

KURTZWEIL
My name's Kurtzweil. Dr. Alvin Kurtzweil.

MULDER
I know the name. Why?

KURTZWEIL
Old friend of your father's.
Kurtzweil continues peeing. Knows this got Mulder's attention.

KURTZWEIL
Back at the Department of State. We were what you might call fellow travelers, but his disenchantment outlasted mine.
(beat)
I never believed in the Project.
Mulder stares at Kurtzweil now. He's being toyed with.
He turns, opens the door into the bar. As Kurtzweil gets a little louder.

KURTZWEIL
Oh, come on. Don't pretend you don't know about the Project. Your father died for it. Your sister was taken because of it.
Kurtzweil finishes nature's call. Zips up. Heads after Mulder.

INT. DOWNSCALE D. C. BAR - NIGHT
Mulder is coming from the back. Kurtzweil moving to catch up. And he does, at the coat stand. The place has pretty much cleared out, except for the Barmaid and some help.

MULDER
How'd you find me?

KURTZWEIL
Heard you come here now and again.

Figured you'd be needing a little drinky tonight.

MULDER
You a reporter?

KURTZWEIL
I'm a doctor, but I think I mentioned that. OB-GYN.

MULDER
Who sent you?

KURTZWEIL
I came on my own. After reading about the bombing in Dallas.

MULDER
Well, if you've got something to tell me, you've got as long as it takes me to hail a cab...
Mulder starts out the door, but Kurtzweil grabs his arm.

KURTZWEIL
They're going to pin Dallas on you,
Agent Mulder. But there was nothing you could've done. Nothing anyone could've done to prevent that bomb from going off. Because the truth is something you'd never have guessed; never have predicted.
Mulder pulls away from Kurtzweil, but Kurtzweil dogs him to:

EXT. STREET OUTSIDE DOWNSCALE BAR - NIGHT
The street is empty, the hour is late. Mulder moves to the curb.

MULDER
And what's that?

KURTZWEIL
S. A. C. Darius Michaud never tried or intended to defuse the bomb.

MULDER
(rhetorical disbelief)
He just let it explode.

KURTZWEIL
What's the question nobody's asking?
Why that building? Why not the Federal
Building?

MULDER
The Federal Building was too well guarded.

KURTZWEIL
No. They put the bomb in the building across the street because it DID have federal offices. The Federal Emergency
Management Agency had a provisional medical quarantine office there. Which is where the bodies were found. But that's the thing...
Mulder's got his hand up for a taxi coming. It's pulling over as Mulder steps from the curb, stepping away from
Kurtzweil.

KURTZWEIL
... the thing you didn't know. That you'd never think to check.
Mulder's got the taxi door open, turning to Kurtzweil.

KURTZWEIL
Those people were already dead.

MULDER
Before the bomb went off?

KURTZWEIL
That's what I'm saying.
Mulder stares at Kurtzweil for a moment.

MULDER
Michaud was a twenty-two year veteran of the bureau --

KURTZWEIL
Michaud was a patriot. The men he's loyal to know their way around Dallas.
They blew that building to hide something. Maybe something even they couldn't predict.

MULDER
You're saying they destroyed an entire building to hide the bodies of three firemen... ?

KURTZWEIL
And one little boy.
Mulder gets in the cab, closes the door. Rolls down the window.

MULDER
I think you're full of shit.

KURTZWEIL
Do you?

Kurtzweil raps the top of the roof and steps away from the car. As the taxi takes off. WE STAY WITH KURTZWEIL, watching Mulder's cab speed away. (NOTE: This should also be covered from inside the cab with Mulder, to play the scene out on him.)

INT. AGENT SCULLY'S BEDROOM - NIGHT
Scully is in bed, lying awake. Staring at the ceiling.
When she reacts to a POUNDING AT HER DOOR.

INT. SCULLY'S APARTMENT - NIGHT
CLOSE ON THE FRONT DOOR. Scully peeks in the peephole.
Then she removes the safety chain, opening the door.

MULDER
(strangely intense)
I wake you?

SCULLY
No.

MULDER
Why not? It's three AM.

Scully gets a whiff of his breath. As he moves past her into the apartment. Radiating a kind of manic intensity.

SCULLY
Are you drunk, Mulder?

MULDER
I was until about an hour ago.

SCULLY
Is that before or after you got the idea to come here?

Mulder looks at her curiously.

MULDER
What are you implying, Scully?

SCULLY
(frowning)
I thought you may have gotten drunk and decided to come here to talk me out of quitting.

MULDER
Is that what you'd like me to do?
Scully hesitates. Long enough to indicate her own wavering heart.

SCULLY
Go home, Mulder. It's late.

MULDER
Get dressed, Scully.

SCULLY
Mulder -- what are you doing?

MULDER
Just get dressed. I'll explain on the way.

EXT. TEXAS FLATLAND - NIGHT
The moon is rising over the horizon, across the curvilinear distance of endless scrub and sagebrush.
When FLYING OBJECTS cross between it and us, their forms unidentifiable in the rising heat waves off the earth.
But they are moving towards us, SILHOUETTES in the background of the moon.
They move silently, their size INCREASING as they move closer. And then we hear them, moments before they arrive at our position, UNMARKED HELICOPTERS just overhead. Hugging the ground as they blast across the dark Texas night.

INT. UNMARKED BLACK HELICOPTERS - NIGHT
Flying at dangerously low altitude over the almost featureless night landscape. Heading for something that we see ahead in the distance. What looks like a LARGE
GLOWING DOME surrounded by the lights of a residential area we've already seen, on the edge of suburban Dallas sprawl.

EXT. SMALL DIRT FIELD - CENTRAL TEXAS - NIGHT
The field where the kids had been digging has been transformed into some kind of worksite.
A LARGE WHITE DOMED TENT has been erected over almost the entire patch of ground, surrounded by the CARGO
TRUCKS that we saw earlier, and more unmarked vans and trucks. There are men in black fatigues moving about, and scientists in haz-mat suits.
As the UNMARKED BLACK HELICOPTERS bank overhead. Coming in for a landing in the glow cast from the tents. CAMERA

MOVING TOWARD one of the helicopters as it lightly touches down and its black door swings open. A man stepping out, and as CAMERA PUSHES UP INTO HIS FACE we recognize him as The Cigarette Smoking Man.

The figure that we've come to know as an assassin and a model of modern self-interest and amorality. One of the central protagonists in the conspiracy to keep the truth from the American people about the existence of extraterrestrial life.

Something known only as: "The Project."

He walks out from under the whirring prop, just far enough to get a flame from his lighter, to get a cigarette lit. As we:

INT. LARGE WHITE TENT - NIGHT - CONTINUOUS

A SCIENTIST in a haz-mat suit is moving through the maze of clear plastic tubing that divides work areas within the tent. Areas where scientists are working at tables doing what appears to be some kind of high-tech archeological work. It is a hive of activity within, as the Scientist leads us past the REFRIGERATION UNITS to the earthen hole where Dr. Bronschweig (we've met him earlier, coming out of a med-evac chopper that landed when the tent city was erected) appears out of the earthen hole, which is reason for all this excitement.

Climbing out A CLEAR HATCH which has been fashioned to cover the hole. Seeing:

THE CIGARETTE SMOKING MAN
Now suited up himself. Bronschweig approaches him.

CIGARETTE SMOKING MAN
You've got something to show me.

DR. BRONSCHWEIG
(nervous excitement)
Yes.

INT. ICE CAVE - CONTINUOUS

What we originally established as icy, and what later became the unfrozen Texas field where the boys discovered the human skull, has been turned to its previously icy state. Thanks to two large vents that Dr.
Bronschweig is pointing at:

DR. BRONSCHWEIG
We brought the atmosphere back down to freezing in order to control the development, which is nothing like we've ever seen.

CIGARETTE SMOKING MAN
Brought on by what?

DR. BRONSCHWEIG
Heat, I think. The coincident invasion of a host, the fireman, and an environment that raised his basic body temperature above ninety eight point six.

They step over to a section of the cave which has been draped with more plastic, the lights from inside this are giving off a cool blue light (passing by TWO
PORTABLE DRILLING RIGS which have been erected, their pumps moving up and down like rocking horses.)

Bronschweig pushes away the plastic, revealing A MAN lying on a gurney draped in plastic. he is hooked up to various and sundry machines which are monitoring his life signs.

His skin has turned almost translucent, the veins and capillaries now clearly visible, as is his pulse. His heartbeat sending life-sustaining blood and energy through his body.

CIGARETTE SMOKING MAN
This man's still alive.

DR. BRONSCHWEIG
Technically and biologically, though he'll never recover.
The CSM is shaking his head in nervous, uneasy wonder.

CIGARETTE SMOKING MAN
How can this be?

DR. BRONSCHWEIG
The developing organism is using his life energy, digesting bone and tissue. We've just slowed the process.
Bronschweig redirects a light so that it shines hard into the man's face and; then we see it. Movement.

CLOSE ON MAN'S FACE
Though the man's eyes still blink occasionally, we can actually see through his tissue and the bones in his skull to see something IS LIVING INSIDE HIM.

ANGLE UP ON CSM AND BRONSCHWEIG
The Cigarette Smoking Man's mind is working intently on all the possibilities, and consequences.

DR. BRONSCHWEIG
Do you want me to destroy this one, too? Before it gestates?

CIGARETTE SMOKING MAN
No. No... we need to try our vaccine on it.

DR. BRONSCHWEIG
And if it's unsuccessful?

CIGARETTE SMOKING MAN
Incinerate it. Like the others.

DR. BRONSCHWEIG
This man's family will want to see the body laid to rest.

CIGARETTE SMOKING MAN
Tell them he was trying to save the young boy's life, and that he died heroically like the other firemen.

DR. BRONSCHWEIG
Of what?

CIGARETTE SMOKING MAN
They seemed to buy our story about the
Hanta virus. You'll make sure the families are taken care of financially, along with a sizeable donation to the community.
(beat)
Maybe a small roadside memorial.
He watches the CSM exit, then back to the prostrate fireman.

CLOSE ON PROSTRATE FIREMAN
There is more movement within his body. Within his chest and neck, as if the creature gestating inside is continuing to stretch and grow. So that now we can see one of its BLACK EYES staring from through the clear flesh of the fireman. An eye which BLINKS at us. As we:

INT. BETHESDA NAVAL HOSPITAL - NIGHT
Mulder and Scully appear at the end of a long hall.
Moving TOWARD CAMERA where a YOUNG NAVAL GUARD sits in f. g. As a LEGEND appears, to establish.
Mulder and Scully moving the long distance to the
Guard's station. Where the Guard looks up at them with military scrutiny.

YOUNG NAVAL GUARD
ID and floor you're visiting.
They both show their FBI IDs.

MULDER
We're going to the morgue.

YOUNG NAVAL GUARD
That area is currently off limits to anyone other than authorized medical personnel.

MULDER
On whose orders?

YOUNG NAVAL GUARD
General McAddie's.
Mulder doesn't miss a beat.

MULDER
General McAddie is who requested our coming here. We were awakened at three AM and told to get down here immediately.

YOUNG NAVAL GUARD
I don't know anything about that.

MULDER
Well, call General McAddie.

YOUNG NAVAL GUARD
I don't have his number.

MULDER
They can patch you in through the switchboard.
The Guard is nervous about this, checking his watch. He picks up the phone, going through a large directory.

MULDER
Hey! We don't have time to dick around here watching you demonstrate your ignorance in the chain of command. The order came direct from General
McAddie. Call him. We'll conduct our business while you confirm authorization.
Mulder is already directing Scully past the Naval Guard who tentatively picks up the phone again.

YOUNG NAVAL GUARD
(to their backs)
Why don't you go on ahead head and
I'll confirm authorization.

MULDER
Thank you.

LEADING Mulder and Scully, moving they've pulled off a con.

MULDER
Why is a morgue suddenly off limits on orders of a general?

INT. BETHESDA NAVAL HOSPITAL - MORGUE FREEZER - NIGHT
TRACKING TABLE HEIGHT across gurneys where white sheet-wrapped bodies lie. CAMERA LANDING ON Scully.
Standing next to Mulder who is undoing the peculiar ropey stitching on the sheet used to secure the bodies.

SCULLY
This is one of the firemen who died in Dallas?

MULDER
According to this tag.

SCULLY
And you're looking for?

SCULLY
I can tell you that without even looking at him.
(off Mulder's look)
Conclusive organ failure due to proximal exposure to source and flying debris.
Scully pulls out an autopsy report that was laid on the gurney under the body of the sheet-wrapped corpse.

SCULLY
This body has already been autopsied,
Mulder. You can tell from the way it's been wrapped and dressed.
Undeterred, Mulder works to get the sheet off. The first thing we notice is that he's still in his fireman's uniform. His face looks familiar to us, not because we know him, but because of the translucency of skin we saw in the other fireman. (We will also notice he's missing an arm, a leg and large part of his torso.)

MULDER
Does this fit the description you just read me, Scully?
Scully comes around, reacting to what she sees.

SCULLY
Oh my God. This man's tissue...

Scully is quickly removing a pair of latex gloves, stretching them on to palpate the man's tissue.

MULDER
It's like jelly.

SCULLY
There's some kind of cellular breakdown. It's completely edematous.
She palpates the spongy skin on the man's face, neck.
Unbuttoning the uniform now, seeing:

SCULLY
And there's been no autopsy performed.
There's no Y incision here; no internal exam.

MULDER
You're telling me the cause of death on the report is false. That this man didn't die from an explosion, or from flying debris.

SCULLY
I don't know what killed this man. I'm not sure if anybody else could claim to either.
Off Mulder's reaction to this:

INT. MORGUE - PATHOLOGY LAB - NIGHT - MINUTES LATER
The gurney with the fireman is pushed through a pair of swinging doors into the darkened lab. Scully flips the lights on, looking around at the giant facility.

SCULLY
(pushing him)
You knew this man didn't die at the bomb site before we got here.

MULDER
I'd been told as much.

SCULLY
You're saying the bombing was a cover-up. Of what?

MULDER
I don't know. But I have a hunch what you're going to find here isn't anything that can be categorized or easily referenced.

SCULLY

Mulder, this is going to take some time, and somebody's going to figure out soon enough we're not even supposed to be here.
(beat)
I'm in serious violation of medical ethics.

MULDER
We're being blamed for these deaths.
Scully, I want to know what this man died of. Don't you?
Scully stares at Mulder, then back down at the body. How can she refuse, given the finality and the personal appeal of the request? After a moment's hesitation, she turns to the body, and to the tray table of tools nearby. Resigned, if not resolved.

EXT. WASHINGTON D. C. - NIGHT
A LEGEND appears: WASHINGTON D. C. , DUPONT CIRCLE. 4:00 AM. The street is fairly empty, save for a garbage truck picking up the stacks of green garbage bags laid out on the sidewalks. Then A TAXI turns off a main street,

MOVING TOWARDS US.
INT. WASHINGTON D. C. STREET - TAXI - NIGHT
OVER MULDER to the street: Where the taxi is moving forward toward a spot where two ARLINGTON PD cruisers are pulled up to the curb. Mulder checks the address he has written down.

MULDER
(to the Cabbie)
I think this is it up here.

EXT. SIDE STREET - NIGHT
The taxi pulls over and Mulder exits, starting up the steps of a walk up where the door is open.

INT. KURTZWEIL'S APARTMENT - NIGHT
There are UNIFORMED OFFICERS inside, and a DETECTIVE.
Mulder steps into an office. FOUR PAIRS of eyes give him the once over. The Detective stepping over to him.

MULDER
Is this Dr. Kurtzweil's residence?

DETECTIVE
(suspiciously)
You got some kind of business with him?

MULDER
I'm looking for him.

DETECTIVE
Looking for him for what?
Mulder pulls out his ID, flashes it at the Detective.

DETECTIVE
(to his partners)
Feds are looking for him, too.
(turns to Mulder)
Real nice business he's got, huh?

MULDER
What's that?

DETECTIVE
Selling naked pictures of little kids over his computer.
Mulder nods, though this is news to him. He steps in a little further, noticing a shelf lined with books. Their spines all have the author's name written large: DR.

ALVIN KURTZWEIL.
Mulder picks up one of these books, with the title: THE

FOUR HORSEMEN OF THE GLOBAL DOMINATION CONSPIRACY.
DETECTIVE
You looking for him for some other reason?

MULDER
Yeah, I had an appointment for a pelvic examination.
They stare at Mulder like he's a sicko. He smiles and they break into RAUCOUS LAUGHTER.

DETECTIVE
You want a call if we turn up Kurtzweil?

MULDER
No. Don't bother.
Mulder puts the book back among the others on the shelf.
And exits. Onto:

RESUME EXT. KURTZWEIL'S APARTMENT - NIGHT

Mulder starting up the street when he notices:

MULDER'S POV
Kurtzweil has stepped from between two apartments. He's staring at Mulder, nodding furtively to him. Then stepping back.

RESUME MULDER
Slows, then speeds up.

EXT. SPACE BETWEEN TWO APARTMENTS - NIGHT
Mulder appears at the end of the narrow walkway, finding Kurtzweil tucked a few yards in.

KURTZWEIL
See this bullshit... ? Somebody knows
I'm talking to you.

MULDER
Not according to the men in blue.

KURTZWEIL
What is it? Kiddie porn again? Sexual battery of a patient? I've had my license taken away in three states.

MULDER
They want to discredit you -- for what?

KURTZWEIL
For what? Because I'm a dangerous man.
Because I know too much about the truth.

MULDER
You mean that apocalyptic trash you write? I knew your name was familiar.
I just didn't know why.

KURTZWEIL
You know my work?

MULDER
(pointedly)
Dr. Kurtzweil, I'm not interested in bigoted ideas about race or genocide.
I don't believe in the Elders of Zion, the Knights Templar, the Bilderburg
Group or in a oneworld Jew run government --

KURTZWEIL

I don't either, but it sure sells books.

He says it with an ironic smile. Causing Mulder to turn and start off. But Kurtzweil hurries to grab him, to prevent this.

KURTZWEIL

I was right about Dallas. Wasn't I, Agent Mulder?

MULDER

How?

KURTZWEIL

I picked up the historical document of the venality and hypocrisy of the American government. The daily newspaper.

MULDER

You said the firemen and the boy were found in the temporary offices of the Federal Emergency Management Agency.
Why?

KURTZWEIL

According to the newspaper, FEMA had been called out to manage an outbreak of the Hanta virus. Are you familiar with the Hanta virus, Agent Mulder?

MULDER

It was a deadly virus spread by field mice in the Southwest U. S. several years ago.

KURTZWEIL

And are you familiar with FEMA? What the Federal Emergency Management Agency's real power is? FEMA allows the White House to suspend constitutional government upon declaration of a national emergency.
To create a non-elected government.
Think about that.
(beat)
What is an agency with such broad sweeping power doing managing a small viral outbreak in suburban Texas?

MULDER

Are you saying it wasn't such a small outbreak?
Kurtzweil is getting intense now.

KURTZWEIL
I'm saying it wasn't the Hanta virus.
They are both given a start when a POLICE CRUISER rolls by on the street, giving a burp of its siren. It rolls past as the two men tuck in tighter.

MULDER
What was it?

KURTZWEIL
When we were young men in the military, your father and I were recruited for a project. They told us it was biological warfare. A virus.
There were rumors about its origins.

MULDER
What killed those men?

KURTZWEIL
What killed them I won't even write about. I tell you, they'd do more than just harass me. They have the future to protect.

MULDER
I'll know soon enough.

KURTZWEIL
(worked up)
What killed those men can't be identified in simple medical terms. My god, we can't even wrap our minds around something as obvious as HIV.
We have no context for what killed those men, or any appreciation of the scale in which it will be unleashed in the future. Of how it will be transmitted; of the environmental factors involved.

MULDER
A plague?

KURTZWEIL
The plague to end all plagues, Agent
Mulder. A silent weapon for a quiet war. The systematic release of an indiscriminate organism for which the men who will bring it on still have no cure. They've been working on this for fifty years. While the rest of the world was fighting gooks and commies these men have been secretly negotiating a planned Armageddon.

MULDER
Negotiating with whom?

KURTZWEIL
I think you know. The timetable has been set. It will happen on a holiday, when people are away from their homes.
When our elected officials are at their resorts or out of the country.
The President will declare a state of emergency, at which time all federal agencies, all government will come under the power of the Federal
Emergency Management Agency. FEMA,
Agent Mulder. The secret government.

MULDER
And they tell me I'm paranoid.

KURTZWEIL
Something's gone wrong -- something unanticipated. Go back to Dallas and dig. Or you're only going to find out like the rest of the country, Agent
Mulder. When it's too late.
Kurtzweil turns, starts off. Mulder stares after him.
Then:

MULDER
How can I reach you?

KURTZWEIL
You can't.
Mulder moves to catch up to Kurtzweil, pulling out his cell phone. Kurtzweil stops, turns. Truly and intensely paranoid. Mulder makes him take the cell phone.

MULDER
No calling Hawaii.
Mulder turns and moves back out onto the street.

INT. MORGUE - PATHOLOGY LAB - NIGHT
Agent Scully wears a surgical mask, latex gloves.
Working on the body of the fireman... when she reacts to a NOISE. Doors opening, closing somewhere o. s. CAMERA
MEDIUM WHIPS to a door where she and Mulder entered the morgue. Where... the Young Naval Guard and TWO MPs push through and enter. They stand looking at:

THEIR POV
Where Scully stood moments ago, there is now just an unattended gurney. A sheet over the fireman's body.
Scully is gone.

RESUME YOUNG NAVAL GUARD, MPs
Tense. Listening, watchful. Moving into the room.

INT. BETHESDA NAVAL HOSPITAL - MORGUE FREEZER - NIGHT
Scully enters the space where she and Mulder found the fireman's body. Trying to quietly click the door shut.
Standing now near the door, tense, listening. When the
CHIRPING of her cell phone breaks the tense silence. She pats frantically at her coat, trying to get it answered before it rings again. Unsuccessfully. Finally getting a hold of it and hitting the send button. Scully sits breathing heavy, nervous breaths -- waiting for the Young Naval Guard to come running in.

MULDER'S VOICE (FILTER)
Scully... ?
She puts the phone slowly up to her face.

SCULLY
(low whisper)
Yeah.

INTERCUT WITH:
INT. PHONE BOOTH - WASHINGTON D. C. - MORNING
Mulder's at the pay phone.

MULDER
Why are you whispering?

SCULLY
I can't really talk right now.

MULDER
What did you find?

SCULLY
Evidence of a massive infection.

MULDER
What kind of infection?

SCULLY
I don't know.

MULDER

Scully -- listen to me. I'm going home, then I'm booking a flight to
Dallas. I'm getting you a ticket, too.

SCULLY
Mulder --

MULDER
I need you there with me. I need your expertise on this. The bomb we found was meant to destroy those bodies and whatever they were infected by.

SCULLY
I've got a hearing tomorrow --

MULDER
-- I'll have you back for it, Scully.
Maybe with evidence that could blow that meeting away.

SCULLY
Mulder -- I can't -- I'm already way past the point of common sense here

--
Scully hears VOICES in the hall outside the freezer.

MULDER
MULDER
Scully... ? Hello... ?
But the line OFF, goes dead. Mulder hangs up the phone, frustrated. Exits the booth in a hurry.

INT. BETHESDA NAVAL HOSPITAL - MORGUE FREEZER - NIGHT
The door opens and the Young Naval Guard steps inside, followed by the MPs. Moving into the room.

LOW ANGLE - TRACKING
with the Naval Guard's feet as they pass by the rolling carts on which bodies are laid. TRACKING to find SCULLY, where she hides under one of the carts. Huddled and cold. The Guard's feet stop near here. He stands motionless for a moment, then moves off. HOLD her until the door slams shut.

INT. FBI OFFICE - DALLAS - MORNING - MULDER
enters a forensics lab with a FIELD AGENT. A LEGEND reads: FBI FIELD OFFICE, DALLAS : 11:20 AM.

FIELD AGENT
You're looking for what amounts to a needle in a haystack. I'm afraid the explosion was so devastating there hasn't been a whole lot we've been able to put together just yet.
They are walking amid BOXES of evidence. STACKS of debris. There are FORENSIC TECHS sorting through this material. It looks like the most tedious and painstaking job in the world.

MULDER
I'm looking for anything out of the ordinary. Maybe something from the
FEMA offices where the bodies were found.

FIELD AGENT
We weren't expecting to find those remains, of course. They went right off to Washington.

MULDER
Was there anything in those offices that didn't go to D. C. ?

FIELD AGENT
Some bone fragments came up in the sift this morning. We thought there'd been another fatality, but we found out FEMA had recovered them from an archeological site out of town.

MULDER
Have you examined them?

FIELD AGENT
No. Just fossils, far as I know.
Mulder is nodding, when both men look off at something that's caught their attention o. s.

MULDER
I'd like this person to take a look, if you don't mind.

THEIR POV - AGENT SCULLY
Standing in the doorway to the lab. She looks at Mulder as if she's come in spite of her misgivings. Moving toward them now.

FIELD AGENT
Let me just see if I can lay my hands on what you're looking for.
The Field Agent nods to Scully as he passes, exiting deeper into the room. Leaving Mulder and Scully by themselves momentarily.

MULDER

You said you weren't coming?

SCULLY
I wasn't planning on it. Particularly after spending a half hour in cold storage this morning. But I got a better look at the blood and tissue samples I took from the firemen.

MULDER
What did you find?

SCULLY
(voice lowering pointedly)
Something I couldn't show to anyone else. Not without more information.
And not without causing the kind of attention I'd just as soon avoid right now.
(off Mulder's look)
The virus those men were infected with contains a protein coat I've never seen before. What it did to them it did extremely fast. And unlike the
AIDS virus or any other aggressive strain, it survives very nicely outside the body.

MULDER
How was it contracted?

SCULLY
That I don't know. But if it's through simple contact of blood to blood, and if it doesn't respond to conventional treatments, it could be a serious health threat.
Mulder's reaction is postponed, or at least subdued by the reappearance of the field agent.

FIELD AGENT
Like I said, these are fossils, and they weren't near the blast center, so they aren't going to tell you much.

SCULLY
May I?
He offers Scully the small glass vials in which the bone fragments have been separated. She takes them, looking at them on her way over to the microscope. Tapping out a tiny fragment onto the viewing bed. She puts her eyes down to the stereoscope eyepieces, then almost immediately looks up at Mulder who translates this look almost instantly.

MULDER
You said you knew the location of the archeological site where these were found.

FIELD AGENT
Show you right on a map.
Off Mulder and Scully's traded looks:

EXT. SMALL PUBLIC PARK - WEST TEXAS - DAY
The domed white tent is still in place, the fleet of trucks and equipment surrounding it unmanned. Several large sound-dampened generators still hum away, but the work being done here would be a mystery to anyone who didn't have access to the tent.

INT. DOMED TENT - DAY
An electric Bobcat-like bulldozer maneuvers a very high tech-looking CLEAR CONTAINER to the edge of the earthen hole. The container has monitors and gauges on it, oxygen tanks and what looks like a circulation refrigeration unit. A self-contained life support system. The inside of the container is covered with a thin layer of frost.
When the small bulldozer gets the container over near the hole, several technicians lift it down off the shovel, hand carrying it toward the hole opening. As Dr.
Bronschweig APPEARS, moving to a ladder that leads down into the hole. He's dressed in a haz-mat suit, with the hood off.

DR. BRONSCHWEIG
I need to have those settings checked and re-set. I need a steady minus two
Celsius through the transfer of the body, after I administer the vaccine.
The men nod to Bronschweig, begin checking the settings as Bronschweig puts his hood on, starts down into the hole, through the clear hatch.

INT. SMALLER ICE CAVE - DAY
The refrigeration vents are still pumping in arctic air when Dr. Bronschweig appears descending a fixed ladder.
It is dark in here, save for the ice blue glow of light coming from the plastic draped area where we saw the fireman acting as an incubator/host for some kind of organism growing inside him.
Bronschweig steps over to this area, moves aside the plastic drapery to enter.

ANGLE INSIDE, PLASTIC LINED AREA
Where the body of the fireman is still inside the quarantine bubble litter in f. g. Bronschweig takes out of his pocket a SYRINGE and an AMPULE. Turning now to the body. Stepping to it. Moving a work light, as he had done for the Cigarette Smoking Man, so that it shines on the face of the fireman. But when he does this,
Bronschweig nearly JUMPS, his breath stolen away.
Reacting to:

ANGLE ON FIREMAN'S BODY
The chest and torso have imploded. It has been turned into a muddy mass of blood-stained jelly; bone and tissue melted into an oozing mass which has sunken due to the fact that the creature which was inside is now gone.

CAMERA WHIPS from Bronschweig to the wall. To the temperature gauge which reads about 6 degrees Celsius.
WHIPPING BACK to Bronschweig who is now panicked.

INTERCUT WITH:
INT. DOMED TENT - DAY
ANGLE DOWN ON EARTHEN HOLE, where the Technicians
Bronschweig was speaking to minutes ago react to
Bronschweig's MUFFLED VOICE. He's down below them in the cave, looking up. Pulling his haz-mat hood off. Yelling up to them.

DR. BRONSCHWEIG
It's gone!

TECHNICIAN
It's what?

OVER THE TECHNICIANS TO BRONSCHWEIG DOWN BELOW
DR. BRONSCHWEIG
It's left the body. I think it's gestated --
Bronschweig is starting up the ladder when something stops him.

RESUME INT. ICE CAVE
CREATURE'S POV OF BRONSCHWEIG
He stands frozen on the ladder, squinting into the darkness.

DR. BRONSCHWEIG
Wait -- I see it --

BRONSCHWEIG'S POV
In the shadows there is movement, the creature edging into the light cast from the draped area. We see it is fully formed -- a replica of the Creature we saw at the opening of our story. Though it does not make any kind of aggressive move. As if, newborn, it is tentative.

RESUME BRONSCHWEIG - CREATURE'S POV
He remains standing on a rung of the ladder for a moment, then takes a gentle step back down to the ground.

DR. BRONSCHWEIG
(nervous wonder)
Oh my god. Oh my god.

TECHNICIAN
You see it?

DR. BRONSCHWEIG
Yes. It's... amazing. You want to get down here --
(sotto to himself)
Jesus Lord... so much for little green men.
Dr. Bronschweig moves shakily to put the syringe in the ampule again... when, suddenly, the Creature STRIKES.

CAMERA RUSHING FORWARD TO BRONSCHWEIG.
MATCH
OVERHEAD ANGLE - OVER THE TECHNICIANS
As the Creature slams into Bronschweig, knocking him out of the line of sight from the top of the earthen hole.
There are SCREAMS OF PAIN from Bronschweig, then they abate.

RESUME INT. ICE CAVE
Bronschweig can be heard, but not clearly seen. He is in the shadows himself now.
Trying to pick himself up, and when he manages to do this, teetering back into the light we see that he is bloodied. He is hurt, injured. Making his way back toward the patch of light that comes from the hole above. Hoping to see that help is on its way, while keeping a watchful, wary and worried eye on the shadows, for another attack by the Creature.

DR. BRONSCHWEIG
Hey -- I need help.
But the Technicians looking down on him offer him nothing of the sort. All they do is quickly close the clear hatch that seals Bronschweig inside the cave.

DR. BRONSCHWEIG
Hey!
But he gets no answer, climbing the ladder shakily. A moment later the first Bobcat shovel-full of dirt falls onto the clear hatch and partially obscures the light.
They are burying Bronschweig alive.

INT. DOMED TENT - DAY
ANGLE DOWN ON BRONSCHWEIG through the glass hatch. His
SCREAMS continue. ADJUSTING to the small bulldozer which is quickly hauling the mound of excavated earth into the hole from which it came. While, all around, there is a hive of activity. Men running everywhere.

RESUME INT. ICE CAVE

Bronschweig reacts in silent horror now, only to turn in further horror when he feels the impending attack of:

THE CREATURE
Right behind and just below him. Its grotesque features in momentary high resolution, BEFORE IT ATTACKS CAMERA.
Over and over, savaging Bronschweig in a violent fury.
Its hideous teeth tearing at his flesh - AT CAMERA - driving him off the ladder where the attack continues in momentary glimpses of teeth, of bloody flesh, and of
OILY BLACK BLOOD being spattered about. At the height of the violence we hear Bronschweig SCREAM.
Matching the wound of this, as we:

EXT. ESTATE SOMEWHERE OUTSIDE LONDON - EARLY EVENING
A CHILD'S SCREAM OF JOY. ENGLISH CHILDREN are playing tag or some kind of children's game in the well-manicured garden of a man who the CAMERA FINDS IN
F. G. -- the man we have come to know as THE
WELL-MANICURED MAN. He is also a member of the syndicate running "The Project", though his venality is cloaked in civility and statesmanship. Right now he's watching the children from the back steps of his mansion, charmed by their game. When he is called by someone o. s.

VALET'S VOICE
Sir -- you have a call.
The Well-Manicured Man turns to see:

HIS VALET
Holds the door. After a moment the W. M. M. enters past the Valet. As the screams of the children continue to rise and fall.

INT. SUBURBAN LONDON ESTATE - A BEAUTIFUL STUDY - EVENING
The Well-Manicured Man enters, picks up a blinking line.
Through a window he can still see the children playing.

WELL-MANICURED MAN
Yes.

CIGARETTE SMOKING MAN
(FILTER)
We have a situation. The members are assembling.

WELL-MANICURED MAN

Is it an emergency?

INTERCUT WITH TIGHT CSM AT INT. KENSINGTON BUILDING (NEXT LOC.)

CIGARETTE SMOKING MAN
Yes. A meeting is set. Tonight in
London, to determine a course.

WELL-MANICURED MAN
Who called this meeting?

CIGARETTE SMOKING MAN
Strughold. He's just gotten on a plane in Tunis.
This pronouncement has the power of ending any further questions. An immediate sense of gravity of the situation. The W. M. M. hangs up, moves to the window where he sees some of the HELP is running from the house. The children have all gathered around a BOY who seems to have hurt himself. He's lifted and being carried by the man who's called the W. M. M. into the house.
Off the Well-Manicured Man's concern, we:

EXT. LONDON STREET - NIGHT
A discreet Town Car pulls up out front an understated building in a better West End neighborhood. A driver exits coming around for the Well-Manicured Man who is already exiting, moving to the building. As a LEGEND appears: KENSINGTON, LONDON: 8:01 PM.

INT. KENSINGTON BUILDING - NIGHT
The Well-Manicured Man is admitted by a Valet. The interior has the well-heeled look of money, or a finely appointed residence that no one lives in. The Valet takes the W. M. M.'s coat.

WELL-MANICURED MAN
Has Strughold arrived?

VALET
They're in the library.
He leads the W. M. M. down a hall, to:

INT. LARGE STATELY LIBRARY - NIGHT
A GROUP OF MEN are standing, looking at something on a
TV monitor. A surveillance video. They turn when the
W. M. M. enters. CAMERA FAVORING A SMALL LEAN MAN with close-cropped hair.

He is at once elegant and imposing with eyes that hold you with laser-like acuity. He is CONRAD STRUGHOLD.

The others are of various ethnicities, tailored and dignified. This might be a collection of U. N. delegates.

Indeed some are.

Their business here, however, doesn't represent anyone's interests but their own. As tipped by the attendance of a GROUP ELDER from the U. S. who we've come to know. But, more importantly, by the Cigarette Smoking Man who holds the VCR remote. He pauses the picture.

STRUGHOLD
We began to worry. Some of us have traveled so far, and you are the last to arrive.

WELL-MANICURED MAN
I'm sorry. My grandson fell and broke his leg.

The non-response to this has the same effect as a reprimand. But the W. M. M. will not apologize of kowtow.

STRUGHOLD
While we've been made to wait, we've watched surveillance tapes which have raised more concerns.

The Well-Manicured Man glances to the TV, sees the frame paused.

HIS POV OF TV MONITOR
Where Mulder and Scully's faces are seen in a hallway that we recognize as the Bethesda Naval Hospital.

RESUME WELL-MANICURED MAN
WELL-MANICURED MAN
More concerns than that?

STRUGHOLD
We've been forced to reassess our role in Colonization by new facts of biology which have presented themselves.

GROUP ELDER
(speaking up)
The virus has mutated.

WELL-MANICURED MAN
On its own?

CIGARETTE SMOKING MAN

Its effect on the host has changed.
The virus no longer just invades the brain as a controlling organism. It's developed a way to modify the host body.

WELL-MANICURED MAN
Into what?

STRUGHOLD
A new extraterrestrial biological entity.
It takes a moment to sink in. The weight of this fact.

WELL-MANICURED MAN
My god...

STRUGHOLD
The geometry of mass infection presents certain conceptual re-evaluations for us. About our place in their Colonization.

WELL-MANICURED MAN
This isn't Colonization, it's spontaneous repopulation. All our work... if it's true, then they've been using us all along. We've been laboring under a lie!

2ND ELDER
It could be an isolated case.

WELL-MANICURED MAN
How can we know?!

STRUGHOLD
We're going to tell them what we've found. What we've learned. Turn over a body infected with the gestating organism.

WELL-MANICURED MAN
In hope of what? Learning that it's true?! That we are nothing more than digestives for the creation of a new race of alien lifeforms?!

STRUGHOLD
Let me remind you who is the new race.
And who is the old.
(beat)
What could be gained by withholding anything from them; By pretending to ignorance? Our knowledge may forestall their plans to step up the timetable.
To start Colonization early.

WELL-MANICURED MAN
And if it doesn't? By cooperating now we're but beggars to our demise! Our ignorance was in cooperating with the
Colonists at all.

STRUGHOLD
Cooperation is our only chance of saving ourselves.

CIGARETTE SMOKING MAN
They still need us to carry out their preparations.

STRUGHOLD
We'll continue to use them as they do us. If only to play for more time, to continue work on our vaccine.

WELL-MANICURED MAN
Our vaccine may have no effect!

STRUGHOLD
Well, without a cure for the virus, we're nothing more than digestives anyway.
All eyes go to the Well-Manicured Man. He is respected, if not the odd man out in this room. But he is all restrained anger now.

WELL-MANICURED MAN
My lateness may have well been absence. A course has already been taken.

CIGARETTE SMOKING MAN
There are complications.
He turns back to the TV monitor where Mulder and Scully remain frozen on the screen.

WELL-MANICURED MAN
Do they know?

CIGARETTE SMOKING MAN
Mulder was in Dallas when we were trying to dispose of evidence. He's gone back there again. Someone has tipped him.

WELL-MANICURED MAN
Who?

CIGARETTE SMOKING MAN
Kurtzweil, we think.

STRUGHOLD
We've allowed this man his freedom.
His books have actually helped us to facilitate plausible denial. Has he outlived his usefulness to us?

WELL-MANICURED MAN
No one believes Kurtzweil or his books. He's a toiler. A crank.

STRUGHOLD
And Mulder?

ELDER
Our new situation makes us vulnerable.
If he learns information as we do, he could jeopardize the Project's secrecy.

2ND ELDER
Control of information means control of Mulder.

CIGARETTE SMOKING MAN
I can control Mulder. I've always controlled Mulder.

STRUGHOLD
This may take another approach.
He says this, casting his look toward the Well-Manicured
Man. A look of cold malevolence. The W. M. M. 's reaction is disdain.

WELL-MANICURED MAN
You can't kill Mulder. He's got too much light on him.

STRUGHOLD
You need not kill a man to destroy him.

WELL-MANICURED MAN
(personalizing the inference)
No, you need only take away what is most precious to him.

HARD
EXT. SMALL PUBLIC PARK - CENTRAL TEXAS - DAY
AGENT SCULLY
She stands against a backdrop of Texas flatland, squinting into the sun. Shaking her head.

SCULLY

I don't know, Mulder...
We are:
WIDE ANGLE REVERSE, TO INCLUDE MULDER, standing in the middle of a park, replete with jungle gyms, playground equipment. All brand spanking new. They are standing right where there had once been a hard scrabble, parched and barren little field. Where the earthen hole had been dug by the young boys. And what had later been the site of so much activity by the group of scientists. But where there's now a park, thick green grass covering the parch of ground, including the spot where the hole had been.

SCULLY
He didn't mention a park.

MULDER
This is where he marked on the map,
Scully. Where he says those fossils were unearthed.

SCULLY
I don't see any evidence of an archeological or any other kind of digsite. Not even a sewer or a storm drain.
Mulder scans the area, confounded. Shaking his head as they walk.

MULDER
You're sure the fossils you looked at showed the same signs of deterioration you saw in the fireman's body in the morgue?

SCULLY
(nodding)
The bone was porous, as if the virus of the causative microbe were digesting it.

MULDER
And you've never seen anything like that?

SCULLY
No. It didn't show up on any of the immunohistochemical tests --
Mulder is listening to all this while looking down at his feet:

MULDER
This looks like new grass to you?

SCULLY
It looks pretty green for this climate.
Mulder stops, kneels, touches the thick green carpet of turf. He digs around, lifting up a corner of a new square.

MULDER
Ground's dry about an inch down.
Somebody just laid this down. Very recently, I'd say.

SCULLY
(looking off)
All the equipment is brand new.

MULDER
No irrigation system. Somebody's covering their tracks.
They both turn, looking at something that's caught their attention on the street where their rental car is parked. Three kids, all of whom we recognize from earlier. Stevie's "friends".
Tooling down the street on new BMX bikes. Reacting to
Mulder's loud WHISTLE. This stops them, staring at
Mulder blankly across the distance.

MULDER
Hey!
They don't answer. Just keep staring, squinting into the sun. Mulder and Scully start walking toward them.

SCULLY
Do you live around here?

2ND BOY
Yeah.
As the Agents approach.

MULDER
You see anybody digging here?
The kids don't answer quickly.

2ND BOY
Not supposed to talk about it.

SCULLY
You're not supposed to talk about it?
Who told you that?

3RD BOY
Nobody.

MULDER
Nobody. Same nobody who put this park in? That new equipment...
(off the boys guilty looks)
They buy you these bikes?
The kids shift uncomfortably.

SCULLY
I think you better tell us.

2ND BOY
We don't even know you.

SCULLY
Well, we're FBI agents.

2ND BOY
You're not FBI agents.

MULDER
How do you know?

2ND BOY
Cause FBI agents wear like suits and goofy ties. And dresses like my mom wears to church. Like on that one show.
Mulder and Scully pull their badges. The kids' mouths drop.

MULDER
Maybe you've been watching too much

TV.
3RD BOY
They all left twenty minutes ago.

4TH BOY
Going that way.
The kids all pointing in the same direction.

EXT. CENTRAL TEXAS HIGHWAY - LATE DAY
As Mulder and Scully's rental car RACES by at high speed.

INT. MULDER AND SCULLY'S RENTAL CAR - DAY - CONTINUOUS
Mulder at the wheel, foot to the floor. Scully's got a map out. The mood is urgent, tense.

MULDER
Unmarked tanker trucks... what are archaeologists hauling out in tanker trucks?

SCULLY
I don't know, Mulder.

MULDER
And where are they going with it?

SCULLY
That's the first question to answer, if we're going to find them.

CUT BACK TO:
EXT. CENTRAL HIGHWAY - LATE DAY
Mulder slows down to a stop. They've come to a three-way intersection in the middle of absolutely nowhere that offers them three choices. The car sits idling for several beats.

RESUME INT. RENTAL CAR
Mulder's got his hand on his face rubbing his eyes.

MULDER
What are my choices?

SCULLY
About a hundred miles of nothing in each direction.

MULDER
Where would they be going?

SCULLY
We've got two choices. One of them is wrong.
They are both looking in different directions. The car idling.

MULDER
You think they went left?

SCULLY
I don't know why I think they went right.
A few moments of silence. Then Mulder steps on the gas and goes straight. Heading out onto the only unpaved road. Accelerating away.
Scully looks at him, wondering. As they bump along at speed. Mulder won't look at her for a few moments. Then, turning to her:

MULDER
Five years together -- how many times have I been wrong.

DISSOLVE TO:
EXT. TEXAS HIGHWAY - NIGHT
HEADLIGHTS appear in the distance on a long, dusty stretch of road. GROWING as they approach, then coming to a stop in a cloud of dust as they move into f. g.
Where a LINE OF FENCEPOSTS, BARBWIRE blocks their path.
As the car brakes, the passenger door opens and Scully exits. A hot Texas wind blows. A dog is BARKING somewhere. Scully walks into the headlight wash, looking at a sign on the fence.
After a moment, the driver's door opens and Mulder exits.

MULDER
Hey, I was right about the bomb, wasn't I?

SCULLY
This is great. This is fitting.

REVERSE ON SCENE
On the fence sign, painted in crude letters, are the words: SOME HAVE TRIED, SOME HAVE DIED. TURN BACK -- NO

TRESPASSING.
MULDER
What?

SCULLY
I've got to be in Washington D. C. in eleven hours for a hearing -- the outcome of which might possibly affect one of the biggest decisions of my life. And here I am standing out in the middle of nowhere Texas, chasing phantom tanker trucks.

MULDER
We're not chasing trucks, we're chasing evidence --

SCULLY
-- of what exactly?!

MULDER
That bomb in Dallas was allowed to go off, to hide something: bodies infected with a virus you detected yourself.

SCULLY

They haul gas in tanker trucks, they haul oil in tanker trucks -- they don't haul viruses in tanker trucks.

MULDER
Yeah, well they may this one.

SCULLY
What do you mean by haul?
(off his reaction)
What are you not telling me here?

MULDER
This virus -- it...
(afraid to say)

SCULLY
Mulder --

MULDER
It may be extraterrestrial.

SCULLY
I don't believe this. I don't fucking believe this.
(reaching her limit of impatience)
Y'know, I've been here... I've been here one too many times with you, Mulder.

MULDER
Been where?

SCULLY
Pounding down some dirt road in the middle of the night. Chasing some elusive truth on a dim hope, only to find myself standing right where I am right now: at another dead end --

As she says this A BELL starts to sound. A flashing light hits Mulder and Scully. They both turn to see:

HIGH ANGLE OVER A RAILROAD CROSSING SIGN
Sitting all by its lonely self. No swinging arms or gate. Just one little sign between Mulder and Scully and their car.
CAMERA PANNING to the light of a locomotive speeding toward us.

WIDE ANGLE OVER TRACKS TO MULDER AND SCULLY

They move toward their car, but the train is coming fast. Mulder and Scully stop and wait, watching the train. As the engine breaks frame, eclipsing Mulder and
Scully from view. And as it passes by we see TWO VERY
FAMILIAR WHITE TANKERS loaded piggyback atop flat bed cars.
The train, which is not much longer than this, passes.
And Mulder and Scully make a mad dash for their car. The lights come on and Mulder swings the vehicle into a hard accelerating turn, taking the spoke of the intersection that parallels the tracks. As the car hauls ass after the train, we:

DISSOLVE TO:
EXT. OPPOSITE END OF MOUNTAIN PASS - NIGHT
The rails come up a grade where they appear out of a long bending turn. Exiting the mountain pass near the summit of the mountain. And now HEADLIGHTS appear, bouncing toward us. It's Mulder and Scully's rental chugging up the grade.
And now pulling to a stop as it REACHES CAMERA. Then the car doors open and Mulder and Scully exit. Putting jackets against the cold desert night. Running over the gravel on the rail bed into sharp f. g.

SCULLY
What do you think it is?

MULDER
I have no idea.
They start out toward it anyway, whatever it is. But the image that we see next might cause us to ask the same question.

REVERSE ANGLE -- MULDER AND SCULLY'S FORMER POV
The Agents are moving off the tracks now, picking their way toward the horizon where, at the edge of the great plateau that lays out before them, there are TWO GIANT

GLOWING WHITE DOMES.
It is otherwise pitch dark out, almost giving the impression that the domes are floating.
It would give the distinct impression of otherworldliness, if we hadn't seen a similar, smaller glowing dome over the dirt field where the boys found the skull. And if we could not see the lights of the
TRAIN rolling to a stop near the mysterious domes.

EXT. GREAT PLATEAU - NIGHT - HIGH WIDE ANGLE
SLOWLY CRANING DOWN as Mulder and Scully move through the low scrub of the high desert. Moving towards us as
CAMERA CONTINUES ITS SLOW CRANE DOWN, REVEALING in f. g. the tops of CORN STALKS (yes, corn stalks.) What is the perimeter edge of:

REVERSE CRANE DOWN (TO MATCH)
Acres and acres of corn fields, laying out before us in the dark night. Running all the way to the WHITE DOMED
TENTS in the b. g.
Mulder and Scully enter the perimeter edge, disappearing into:

EXT. ACRES OF CORN - NIGHT
TRACKING WITH Mulder and Scully as they move through the field.

SCULLY
This is weird, Mulder.

MULDER
Very weird.

SCULLY
Any thoughts on why anybody'd be growing corn in the middle of the desert?

MULDER
Not unless those are giant Jiffy Pop containers out there.
CONTINUE TRACKING as they move through the tall uniform rows.

ANGLE BEHIND THE AGENTS
Shooting down the long straight rows. CRANING UP to
REVEAL DOMES once again. Like space ships that have landed.

OPPOSITE PERIMETER OF THE FIELD OF CORN
The Agents exit the edge of the crop field. They have come upon the glowing tents now. Tall and pillowy against the dark sky.
There is no evidence of anyone about. No sound, no signs.
Mulder and Scully stand at the edge of the field for a moment. Then move cautiously across an open area to one of the domes.

INT. WHITE DOME TENT - NIGHT
Mulder pulls open the steel door leading in. It opens with a SUCKING SOUND which suggests the interior is pressurized. And as he and Scully step in -- they both
JUMP when LARGE FANS just overhead hit them both with hard blasts of air.
Stepping quickly out of the downward blasting air, into the still silence of the space beyond.

SCULLY
Cool in here. Temperature's being regulated.

MULDER
For the purpose of what?

HIGH OVERHEAD ANGLE
Our view is down through the crosswires and cables that create the tension support. The effect is a combination of simplicity and perfect function. Stark and high tech.
The flooring is gray and flat, featureless. But we don't yet see from this angle exactly what the white domed tent houses.
Though the air is still and there is no movement of any kind, there is a sound that permeates the interior. A
STEADY HUM. Almost electrical hum, but different.
Mulder and Scully move together toward the middle of the space.

WIDE ON TENT - MULDER AND SCULLY'S POV
Laid out in a grid, low to the ground, are what look like BOXES. Fixed in place like roof vents, except these are on the floor, no more than three feet tall, and about the same measure square.

NEW ANGLE - TRACKING WITH MULDER AND SCULLY
As they continue to move cautiously, walking out into the grid of box-shaped objects. Coming to the center of the capacious, arena-sized space. Standing over one of the mysterious boxes, which we now see have LOUVERED
TOPS. The louvers, however, are shut so that whatever is inside the boxes cannot be seen.

SCULLY
I think we're on top of something. I think these are some kind of venting.
Mulder lays his head and ear to the top of the box.

MULDER
You hear that?

SCULLY
I hear the humming. Like electricity.
High voltage maybe.

MULDER
Maybe. Maybe not.
Scully looks skyward.

SCULLY
What do you think those are for?
Mulder takes his ear off the box, looking up now, too.

THEIR POV
At the top of the dome are two LARGE corresponding

LOUVER VENTS.
RESUME MULDER AND SCULLY
Looking up at these vents.

INT. WHITE DOME TENT - NIGHT
HIGH WIDE ANGLE OVER MULDER AND SCULLY, staring up JUST
PAST CAMERA at the louvered vents at top center of the tent. When A LOUD
METALLIC NOISE makes them jump.

AGENTS POV THE LOUVERED VENTS ABOVE THEM
One of the vents is opening automatically, its large metal louvers straining from their flat closed position into an up-and-down open position. When this is complete, the SECOND LOUVER does the same.
The straining sound of galvanized metal-on-metal.

LOW ANGLE ON MULDER AND SCULLY
As Mulder turns his look from the ceiling back down to the mysterious box they're standing next to. Something occurs to him. Something frightening.

MULDER
Scully.... ?

SCULLY
Yeah... ?

MULDER
Run.
Mulder grabs her hand, pulling her along. Though she doesn't know why. Or what's about to happen. TRACKING
FAST WITH THEM as Mulder leads her back toward the door they entered, which is a good hundred yards away.

SCULLY
(yelling, on the run)
What are you doing?

MULDER
(yelling back)
Come on!

When the LOUVERED VENTS on all the low grid-arranged boxes OPEN IN DOMINO-LIKE SUCCESSION -- out of them pouring THOUSANDS AND THOUSANDS OF BEES, rapidly filling the atmosphere of the domed space.
As if the insects are being shot out of non-stop cannons.

HIGH ANGLE
THICK STREAMS of bees head RIGHT AT CAMERA, flying for the open louvers at the top of the dome. As Mulder and
Scully run for it down below.

TRACKING WITH MULDER AND SCULLY
Scully's hand slipping from Mulder's as she pulls her jacket up over her head. Mulder doing the same now, ducking his head inside his own jacket. The Agents are slowed by the bees but still make their zigzag way toward the door -- bees clinging to their clothes. But motion seems to be the key.
As Mulder RUNS TOWARD CAMERA -- where the downward blast of air knocks all the bees off him. In the b. g. , we see that Scully has fallen behind. Still running, but losing her way in the process, losing her bearings as the thickening swarm of bees descends.

CLOSE ON SCULLY
When Mulder enters frame, jacket pulled over his head again. Taking Scully by the back of her coat and swinging her toward the direction of the door.
Whipsnapping her the rest of the distance to the doorfans. Following right behind her as the fans
BLASTING them and the Agents continue right out the doors. To:

EXT. WHITE DOMED TENT - NIGHT
Scully and Mulder comes blasting out themselves now, but they haven't even had time to catch their breaths when they react to MOVEMENT. Something coming at them in the night.

THEIR POV'S - STRAIGHT DOWN THE ROWS OF DOMED TENTS
Where BRIGHT BEAMS BLAST ON, moving fast toward them.
The RUSHING WHIR of the turbine engines of the unmarked choppers. The bright beams skimming across the ground toward Mulder and Scully, traveling right along the edges of ends of the white domed tents. Threatening to spot the Agents, unless they -- RUN.
And they do -- bolting just as the beams and the helicopters blast over the spot they held just moments before. Running to:

EXT. ACRES OF CORN - NIGHT - MULDER AND SCULLY - VARIOUS HANDHELD

Running flat out now, knocking away the stalks and leaves that block their way.
Following and leading shots.
POVs and Tracking shots.
And chasing angles, as the Agents run through the only cover they've got. As:

ANGLE JUST OVER THE TOP OF CROPS
The unmarked helicopters swoop right overhead, their
BRIGHT SPOTLIGHTS searching and cutting through the cornrows. As the Agents zig and zag just out of the discovering beams. As the choppers zoom right over their heads.

REVERSE ON CHOPPERS
Traversing the field, then doing sharp banking turns and swooping back over the field now in low drifting hovers.
The wash from the blades knocking the corn stalks down so as to reveal anything hidden within.
The bright spots making sure that nothing might escape detection.

LOW ANGLE - CAMERA SEARCHING AND FINDING SCULLY
as she runs up INTO FRAME. She's lost sight of:

SCULLY
Mulder?!

ANGLE ELSEWHERE ON MULDER
As he too runs to a stop. Hearing his name.

MULDER
Scully?!

RESUME SCULLY
Reacting to the sound of her name, but there's no time to find her bearings on Mulder. Not before she has to take flight again. As one of the choppers appears overhead, hovering into view. Knocking the corn down in a path moving straight toward her.
CAMERA LEADING HER as she runs from the oncoming craft.
PASSING CAMERA to the left, as the chopper passes CAMERA

RIGHT.
TRACKING FAST WITH MULDER
Beating his way through the corn like Bomba through the jungle.
Matching this action, as Mulder runs toward us. When one of the unmarked helicopters BREAKS INTO FRAME in an intersecting path, its BEAM passing right over Mulder and ILLUMINATING HIM. But while it doesn't slow Mulder down, the helicopter

maneuvers into a hard banking turn, sweeping over the far end of the corn field and heading

RIGHT BACK AT MULDER - AT US.
NEW LOW ANGLE ON EDGE OF CORN FIELD
Where Mulder bursts out of the perimeter, turning on a quick dime and running an out pattern, just before the chopper BURSTS into frame overhead, its search beam narrowly missing Mulder.

NEW ANGLE ON MULDER
Running the corner of the field, looking frantically down each corn row until he comes to a stop. No sign of:

MULDER
Scully?!
Mulder reacting to the sound of her response:

SCULLY
(distant o. s.)
Mulder!

NEW ANGLE ON SCULLY
She's exiting the field behind him. Running toward him, and when she gets to him they both break into a run across the desert. CAMERA FOLLOWING THEM as they sprint away.
FOLLOWING THEM until they both start to slow. Slowing to a stop in the darkness. Turning to see:

THEIR POV
The helicopters have disappeared.

RESUME MULDER AND SCULLY
Reacting to this.

SCULLY
Where'd they go?

MULDER
I don't know.
Then they both turn again and continue running. As fast as their feet will take them. Back towards the bluff where their car is parked.

EXT. BLUFF OVERLOOKING CORN FIELDS - NIGHT

Where Mulder and Scully's car is parked. Stillness, until Mulder and Scully's heads appear as they climb up from the direction of the corn fields. They get in their car and start it quickly. Mulder turns the ignition, but the car doesn't start immediately. He turns it over and over but it won't kick.

As he does this, unbeknownst to the agents ONE OF THE

BLACK HELICOPTERS rises up from below the bluff, appearing in their rear windshield. Hovering just behind the car like a giant bumblebee. Just as...

... Mulder gets the car started, throwing the transmission in gear and spinning the tires. As they head off back in the direction they came, without their lights on. As they do this, the black chopper continues to hover for a moment, then BANKS OFF AND AWAY. Into the night.

Mulder and Scully speed off in the opposite direction.

As we:

DISSOLVE TO:
INT. FBI OFFICE OF PROFESSIONAL REVIEW - DAY
CLOSE ON A FILE

Being leafed through by a woman's hands. CAMERA TILTING

UP to Special Agent Cassidy, the woman we met earlier running the OPR hearing. She takes a quick glance at her watch, looking up when:

THE DOOR TO THE ROOM

opens. A beat, then Skinner enters with a wearied look.

SKINNER
She's coming in.
Skinner ducks his head back out to look at:

INTERCUT WITH:
INT. HALLWAY OUTSIDE OPR HEARING ROOM - DAY

Where Scully stands looking into the glass of a display case, trying to put her hair and clothes and person together. She's still in the same clothes we saw her in.

Seeing Skinner now moving toward him.

RESUME OPR HEARING ROOM

Scully enters past Skinner. Though she has straightened them, and her hair, there is no mistaking that she's been to the dust bowl and back to get here. Her manner is chastened. Scully tries to keep her eyes on the table where she'll be sitting. Venturing only a brief, polite look to:

ANGLE TO INCLUDE CASSIDY AND THE OTHER PANEL MEMBERS

They reshuffle their papers, pulling up their chairs.

Ready to get down to business now.

CASSIDY
Special Agent Scully --

SCULLY
I apologize for making you wait --
I've brought some new evidence with me

--
CASSIDY
Evidence of what?

CLOSE PROFILE ON SCULLY
Reaching into her satchel, pulling out an evidence bag.
Whatever she's reaching for she's reluctant to present with confidence.

SCULLY
These are fossilized bone fragments
I've been able to study, gathered from the bomb site in Dallas...
As Scully speaks we see A BEE crawl out from under the collar of her suit jacket, crawling toward the back of her neck. Crawling slowly, as if stretching its legs from its long journey. CAMERA DOLLYING around Scully as the bee does, moving into an OVER to:

CASSIDY
You've been back to Dallas?

SCULLY
Yes.

CASSIDY
Are you going to let us in on what exactly you're trying to prove --

SCULLY
That the bombing in Dallas may have been to destroy the bodies of those firemen, so their deaths and the reason for them wouldn't have to be explained --

CASSIDY
(challenging)
-- those are very serious allegations,
Agent Scully --

SCULLY

Yes. I know.

There is a hush of murmured responses to this, the panel members speaking to one another. Assistant Director
Skinner shifts uneasily in his chair. He's been here before with Agents Mulder and Scully. He's sensing something outrageous.

CASSIDY

And you have conclusive evidence of this? Something to tie this claim of yours to the crime --

SCULLY
(grudgingly)
Nothing completely conclusive --

We have returned to the OVER ANGLE on Scully, where we see the BEE just below her jacket collar on the back of her neck.
It CRAWLS back under her collar, DISAPPEARING from sight.

SCULLY

I hope to. We're working to develop this evidence --

CASSIDY

Working with?

SCULLY

Agent Mulder.

Off Cassidy's knowing nod, a general shifting in chairs, we:

INT. DOWNSCALE D. C. BAR - LATE DAY

Mulder pushes through the front, scanning the room for:

ANGLE ON KURTZWEIL

Sitting at a booth at the dark rear of the establishment. Mulder enters frame, sitting down across from him. Kurtzweil is jumpy, but he sees from Mulder's expression that something's up.

KURTZWEIL

You found something?

MULDER

Yes. On the Texas border. Some kind of experiment. Something they excavated was brought there in tanker trucks.

KURTZWEIL

What?

MULDER
I'm not sure. A virus --

KURTZWEIL
-- You saw this experiment?

MULDER
What did it look like?

MULDER
There were bees. And corn crops.
Kurtzweil smiles at Mulder, laughs with nervous excitement. Mulder doesn't quite realize it yet, but this is news to him.

MULDER
What are they?
Kurtzweil slides from his seat, rising.

KURTZWEIL
What do you think?

MULDER
A transportation system. Transgenic crops. The pollen genetically altered to carry a virus.

KURTZWEIL
That would be my guess.

MULDER
Your guess?
But Kurtzweil doesn't respond to this. He's moving toward the back of the bar. Mulder slides out, pursuing him.

ANGLE ON BARMAID
The few PATRONS sitting at the bar, all turning in reaction to this sudden flurry of activity.

INT. REAR OF DOWNSCALE BAR - NIGHT - CONTINUOUS
Near the bathrooms. Mulder catches up to Kurtzweil.

MULDER
What do you mean, your guess?

Kurtzweil doesn't stop. So Mulder must physically stop him.

MULDER
You told me you had answers.

KURTZWEIL
Yeah, well I don't have them all.

MULDER
You've been using me --

KURTZWEIL
I've been using you?!

MULDER
You didn't know my father --

KURTZWEIL
I told you -- he and I were old friends --

MULDER
You're a liar. You lied to me to gather information for you. For your goddamn books. Didn't you?
Mulder is getting heated, rough with Kurtzweil. When, unexpectedly A MAN suddenly exits the bathroom. REACTING to this scene. Kurtzweil uses the moment to break from Mulder. Slipping out the back door. Mulder takes a beat, then goes after him.
Pushing out the back door into the blinding brightness.

EXT. ALLEY BEHIND BAR - DAY
Mulder busts out the back door, chasing Kurtzweil.

MULDER
Kurtzweil!
Kurtzweil turns to him. With restrained ferocity.

KURTZWEIL
You'd be shit out of luck if not for me. You saw what you saw because I led you to it. I'm putting my ass on the line for you.

MULDER
Your ass? I just got chased across
Texas by two black helicopters.

KURTZWEIL
And why do you think it is you're standing here talking to me? These people don't make mistakes, Agent
Mulder.
And with that he turns now, striding off. Leaving Mulder to deal with the excellent logic of this. When suddenly
Mulder reacts to A NOISE. Somewhere above him.

MULDER'S POV
Up on a fire escape, A MAN is moving. Mulder can only see his feet and legs from this angle, but it is clear he has been watching Mulder. Upon being spotted, the figure slides away and disappears.

ANGLE FROM INSIDE FIRE ESCAPE BUILDING
We get a glimpse of the man who was watching him. A face we recognize as that of the man who brushed past Mulder coming out of the vending room, not long before the building in Dallas blew. He is moving quickly now, disappearing into the shadows.
CAMERA TILTING DOWN to find:
MULDER. He stands staring up, but only for a moment until he turns and hurries off in the opposite direction
Kurtzweil disappeared in.

INT. MULDER'S APARTMENT - MAGIC HOUR
ANGLE OVER MULDER'S DESK at the far end of the living room. The sound of keys in the door, then Mulder enters his apartment in a hurry. Moving to the desk and going at this pace through the drawers. Looking for... A

PICTURE ALBUM.
Which he takes now, leafing through it. Flipping the pages, looking for:

ANGLE OVER MULDER
Finding old pictures of young Fox Mulder with his
SISTER, Samantha. With his father and mother. The plastic-covered page is peeled back and one of these photos is removed. It is an old family snapshot. A picnic possibly.
Mulder stares at the picture.
INSERT PHOTO - In the b. g. of the picnic, his head turned to camera, is a young KURTZWEIL.
Mulder studies the photo intensely, when there's a KNOCK at his door. Mulder turning to see:

SCULLY
In his haste, Mulder had neglected to lock his door.

Scully is pushing it open. She's still in the same clothes. She looks beat. Her eyes meeting Mulder's. A gaze that says bad news.

MULDER
What? What's wrong?

SCULLY
Salt Lake City, Utah. Transfer effective immediately.
Mulder is shaking his head. Not wanting to hear this.

SCULLY
I already gave Skinner my letter of resignation.

MULDER
You can't quit, Scully.

SCULLY
I can, Mulder. I debated whether or not to even tell you in person, because I knew --

MULDER
We're close to something here -- we're on the verge --

SCULLY
You're on the verge, Mulder -- please don't do this to me --

MULDER
After what you saw last night -- after all you've seen -- you can't just walk away --

SCULLY
I have. I did. It's done.

MULDER
Just like that --

SCULLY
I'm contacting the state board Monday to file medical reinstatement papers

--
MULDER
I need you on this, Scully --

SCULLY
You don't Mulder -- you've never needed me. I've only held you back.

(beat)
I've got to go.
And with that she exits his apartment, the argument too painful, and her ability to be persuaded too clear to herself.

INT. HALLWAY OUTSIDE MULDER'S APARTMENT - NIGHT
WIDE ANGLE FROM END OF HALL where we see Scully, leaving Mulder's apartment. Moving at a hurried clip to the elevator -- TOWARD CAMERA. As if anticipating her own impulse to turn around and go back. As she moves into f. g. Mulder exits his apt. door.

MULDER
You're wrong --
He hurries to catch her. As she turns on him.

SCULLY
Why was I assigned to you? To debunk your work. To reign you in. To shut you down.

MULDER
You saved me, Scully.
(off her look)
As different and frustrating as it's been sometimes, your goddamn strict rationalism and science have saved me a thousand times; have kept me honest and made me whole. I owe you so much,
Scully, and you owe me nothing.
(beat)
I don't want to do this without you. I don't know if I can. If I quit now, they win.
She is silent, moved. In spite of all her desire not to be. She moves to Mulder, holds him. They break slightly and she looks up at Mulder with deep respect, admiration and... kisses him on the forehead. When...
... suddenly a physical intimacy we've never seen. A heat and passion that can't be denied. The opportunity for the inevitable has presented itself.
The moment of truth has arrived. Mulder is staring at
Scully as she's looking back at him. His head moves slightly toward hers -- as one of his hands moves up to her neck, drawing her to him. Where there is hesitation on her part, there is also desire. When:

SCULLY
OUCH!!!
Scully pulls away from Mulder, RUBBING at her neck where his hand had been.

MULDER
What? What happened?

SCULLY
I think... something stung me.

Scully's hand comes out with THE SQUIRMING BEE, which she holds in her hand while Mulder moves around her, checking her neck.

MULDER
It must...

But he doesn't finish his sentence before he has to catch Scully from falling. Her head bobs and she has to catch it.

MULDER
Scully...

SCULLY
Something's wrong...
(fighting for clarity)
I'm having -- lancinating pain -- my chest. My... motor functions are being affected. I'm...

Mulder lays her down on the floor during this. Scully continues to speak, though her eyes are not focusing.
She is limp in Mulder's arms.

SCULLY
... my pulse feels thready and I've got a funny taste in the back of my throat.

MULDER
I think you're in anaphylactic shock

--
SCULLY
No -- it's --

Her voice is getting thin now, too.

MULDER
Scully --

SCULLY
I've got no allergy. Something... this... Mulder... I think... I think you should call an ambulance.

And Mulder is on his feet in a flash, running for:

INT. MULDER'S APARTMENT - NIGHT - CONTINUOUS

CLOSE OVER PHONE as Mulder races into the apartment, dashing TOWARD CAMERA, picking up the receiver, dialing.
HOLDING ON THE PHONE during this action. TILTING UP for:

MULDER
This is Special Agent Fox Mulder. I have an emergency -- I have an agent down --

INT. HALLWAY OUTSIDE MULDER'S APARTMENT - NIGHT
SCULLY - HANDHELD
Picked up and one-two-three loaded on a gurney by TWO

PARAMEDICS.
1ST PARAMEDIC
Can you hear me? Can you say your name?
Scully is trying, but the words won't come out.

1ST PARAMEDIC
She's got constriction in the throat and larynx -- are you breathing okay?
He lays his head down to her mouth.

1ST PARAMEDIC
Passages are open. Let's get her in the van --
NEIGHBORS are in the hall now, along with Mulder. Who is moving beside the Paramedics as they hustle the gurney down the hall.

1ST PARAMEDIC
Coming through people -- here we go.
Coming through --

EXT. MULDER'S APARTMENT - NIGHT - CONTINUED HAND HELD
The Paramedics bang out the front door, stutter-stepping the gurney down to the walk, to their EMT VAN which sits at the curb with the LIGHT BAR FLASHING. Mulder following close by.

MULDER
She said she had a taste in the back of her throat -- there was no pre-existing allergy to bee-stings -- the bee that stung her may have been carrying a virus --

2ND PARAMEDIC
A virus?

1ST PARAMEDIC

Get on the radio, tell them we have a cytogenic reaction, we need an advise and administer --
They get her to the back of the vehicle, guiding the gurney in with experienced hands. Scully's eyes are on
Mulder as she's slid into the brightly lit interior.
The 1st Paramedic blocks Mulder somewhat as he steps toward the van, anticipating that he's going with them to the hospital. But the doors are closing on him before he gets an opportunity.
FOLLOWING MULDER around to the driver's side of the van now, moving to the driver's window where THE DRIVER can be seen in the rear view mirror, his eyes watching
Mulder.

ON MULDER
A moment of vague recognition -- a catch in his step.

RESUME
As Mulder's momentum carries him to the driver's window where se see again the man from the vending room, who was also surveilling Mulder. And he has a HANDGUN pointed at Mulder, which he FIRES THROUGH THE WINDOW.
The glass shattering.

RESUME MULDER
Throwing himself away backward, but the bullet catches him in the head. Blood and glass spraying onto the side of the van. He goes down to the ground -- as the paramedic van accelerates fast away.

LOW ANGLE REVERSE ON MULDER
Lying in the street, his head bleeding profusely. While in the b. g. , A SECOND AMBULANCE IS SPEEDING TO THE
SCENE. As it skids to a stop and TWO NEW PARAMEDICS jump out, we:

DISSOLVE TO:
EXT. WASHINGTON NATIONAL AIRPORT - NIGHT
A MEDIUM SIZED PRIVATE JET is taxiing down an alley off the main runway where a 747 is speeding toward takeoff.
The private jet turning TOWARD CAMERA and nosing into f. g.

NEW ANGLE ON TARMAC
Where MEN IN FAMILIAR BLACK FATIGUES are unloading something from an unmarked cube truck that is also familiar: the very high tech-looking CLEAR CONTAINER, with its monitors and gauges, its oxygen tanks and refrigeration unit. A

self-contained life support system. The inside of the container is covered with a thin layer of frost, through which we can see AGENT

SCULLY.
She lies as if in a state of paralysis, but a blink of her eyes is enough to tell us that she is... alive.
TRACKING WITH THE MEN moving the container. As they hustle it to the waiting jet. As The Cigarette Smoking
Man is descending the steps of the plane onto the tarmac. Watching as the container is moved to the cargo hold and loaded inside.
The hold is closed and the jet engines wind back up. As the Cigarette Smoking Man reboards the aircraft and it taxis away.

FADE SLOWLY TO BLACK
INT. HOSPITAL - NIGHT
Voices fade in slowly, inaudible at first. For regular viewers of the show, they will recognize the voices of the Lone Gunmen.
Three nerdish paranoiacs who publish a magazine which charts and cataloged conspiracies past and present, among other government malfeasance. They are Langly, Byers and Frohike.

BYERS
I think he's coming out --

LANGLY
He's coming to.

FROHIKE
Hey, Mulder...
FADE UP, as if our eyes are blinking open. We are in
Mulder's POV, and the face right above us is Frohike's.

FROHIKE
Mulder... ?
Behind Frohike, looking down at Mulder, are Byers and
Langly.

REVERSE ON MULDER
Staring at the diminutive Frohike, the long-haired
Langly and the courtly Byers with dawning recognition.

MULDER
Oh god...

LANGLY
What's wrong?

MULDER
(to Byers, then Langly)
Tin Man. Scarecrow.
(to Frohike)
Toto.
Mulder sits up now, rubbing his face, feeling the BANDAGE he's got on his head.

MULDER
What am I doing here?

BYERS
You were shot in the head. The bullet broke the flesh on your right brow and glanced off your temporal plate.

MULDER
(woozy)
Penetration but not perforation.

LANGLY
Three centimetres to the left and we'd be playing the harp.
Mulder is still shaking out the cobwebs.

BYERS
They gave you a craniotomy to relieve the pressure from a subdural hematoma. But you've been unconscious since they brought you in.

MULDER
When was that?

FROHIKE
Two days ago. Your guy Skinner's been here with you around the clock.

LANGLY
We got the news and made a trip to your apartment. Found a bug in your phone line.

FROHIKE
And one in your hall.

Byers holds up the first small device. Frohike holds up a vial containing A BEE. Mulder realizing:

MULDER
Scully had a violent reaction to a bee sting --

BYERS
You called 911. Except the call was intercepted.

MULDER
(sitting up)
They took her --
Mulder pushes the covers off. Swinging his legs to the ground. As A. D. Skinner enters the room. Surprised to see Mulder up.

SKINNER
Agent Mulder --

MULDER
Where's Scully?!
As he says this he loses his balance slightly, has to hold onto one of the Gunmen. Struggling with his faculties.

SKINNER
She's missing. We've been unable to locate her or the vehicle they took her in.

MULDER
Whoever they are -- this goes right back to Dallas -- it goes right back to the bombing --

SKINNER
I know.
(off Mulder's reaction to this)
Agent Scully reported your suspicions to OPR. On the basis of her report, I sent techs over to S. A. C. Michaud's apartment. They picked up PSTN residues on his personal effects consistent with the construction of the vending machine device in Dallas.

MULDER
(reeling)
How deep does this go?

SKINNER
I don't know.

Mulder sees A MAN IN A SUIT passes by the small window in the door, casting a furtive glance in, then moving off. He turns his look back to Skinner.

MULDER
Are we being watched?

SKINNER
I'm not taking any chances.
Mulder nods. Pulling now at the bandage on his head.
Peeling it away and revealing the wound beneath.

MULDER
I need your clothes, Byers.

BYERS
Me?

SKINNER
What are you doing?

MULDER
I've got to find Scully.

FROHIKE
Do you know where she is?

MULDER
No. But I know someone who might have an answer. Who better.
Mulder is undoing his hospital gown now, his white buns gracing the screen for the first time in history. As he ducks into the bathroom. As the men left standing in the room all look to Byers, reluctantly removing his duds.
Off this:

INT. HOSPITAL HALLWAY - NIGHT
ANGLE OVER MAN IN A SUIT standing with his back to
Mulder's room, reading a section of a newspaper (the rest of the paper sitting on a chair, as if the man's possibly set up here.) As the door to Mulder's room opens in the b. g. and Frohike appears.
Frohike keeps his eyes on the Man as Langly appears now, followed by... Byers? We can't see clearly as the other two block our POV and the third man out doesn't show us his face. The threesome starts down the hall, their footsteps drawing the attention of the Man in a Suit.

ANGLE OVER MULDER AND THE OTHER GUNMEN
As they head TOWARD CAMERA. Walking at a pace. In the b. g. the Man in the Suit is drifting toward Mulder's hospital room.

ANGLE ON MAN IN SUIT
Suspicious. He moves to the door, looks in the little glass window. Seeing... Byers, the sheets pulled up to his nose to hide his beard and mustache. Skinner standing next to him, talking on the phone.
The Man in the Suit looking down to the end of the hall again.

RESUME ANGLE OVER MULDER AND THE GUNMEN
As Mulder and his two flankers MOVE RIGHT TO CAMERA.
Mulder is taking a cell phone being handed to him by
Frohike. Dialing on the move.

EXT. ALLEY BEHIND DOWNSCALE D. C. BAR - NIGHT
A FIGURE appears at the end of the alley, moving toward us. It could be Mulder from this distance, but as the figure comes closer we recognize him as Kurtzweil.
Moving into the f. g. , checking behind him, ahead of him.
Jumpy.
He takes a cautious beat, then moves to the door leading into the bar (established), reaching for the knob.
Opening it, finding the Well-Manicured Man standing there.

WELL-MANICURED MAN
Dr. Kurtzweil, isn't it? Dr. Alvin
Kurtzweil?

KURTZWEIL
Jesus Christ.
Kurtzweil is shaken by the sight of this man.
Backpedaling a bit, looking around and behind him for an ambush.

WELL-MANICURED MAN
You're surprised. Certainly you've been expecting some response to your indiscretion.
The W. M. M. steps out of the doorway, following
Kurtzweil.

WELL-MANICURED MAN
I'm quite sure whatever you told Agent
Mulder, you have your good reason.
It's a weakness in men our age; the urge to confess.
(stopping his walk)

I forgive you that.
Kurtzweil is thrown by the words, and the delivery.
Stopping his backward progress. Studying this upright and civil man.

KURTZWEIL
What are you doing here? What do you want from me?

WELL-MANICURED MAN
You must try to understand, what I'm here to do is only to protect my children. You and I have but short lives left. I can only hope the same isn't true for them.
On this note, Kurtzweil turns and hoofs it back in the direction from which he came. TRACKING BACK WITH HIM until HEADLIGHTS hit his face.

REVERSE ANGLE
A TOWN CAR has pulled into the alley behind him.
Accelerating fast down the narrow corridor. Effectively trapping Kurtzweil in. As he squints into its headlights, then turns back with fear in his eyes to the

W. M. M.
EXT. STREET OUTSIDE DOWNSCALE BAR - NIGHT
Where a figure is coming down the street toward us.
Running, it's Mulder, going balls out. Running to the entrance of the bar and yanking open the door.

INT. DOWNSCALE D. C. BAR - NIGHT
Moderately crowded as Mulder enters, stopping to catch his breath. Moving to the back of the bar. Looking for:

THE BOOTH WHERE HE MET KURTZWEIL EARLIER
It's empty.

RESUME MULDER
Moving through the bar -- real panic in his expression.
He heads to the back.

INT. REAR OF DOWNSCALE BAR - NIGHT - CONTINUOUS
Mulder passing the bathrooms, moving to the door where we saw the Well-Manicured Man standing just a short bit ago. But there is no one back here now. Mulder moves to the back door, the one leading to the alley, pushing it open and finding:
The Well-Manicured Man stands with HIS DRIVER closing the trunk on the idling Town Car (which has been turned around.) The W. M. M. turns to see:

WELL-MANICURED MAN

Mr. Mulder.

MULDER
What happened to Kurtzweil?

WELL-MANICURED MAN
He's come and gone.
The W. M. M. moves to Mulder, who doesn't trust him for a second. Mulder is still breathing hard, sizing up this scene.

MULDER
Where's Scully?

WELL-MANICURED MAN
I have answers for you.

MULDER
Is she alive?

WELL-MANICURED MAN
Yes.
Mulder stares at the W. M. M. - measuring him.

WELL-MANICURED MAN
I'm quite prepared to tell you everything, though there isn't much you haven't guessed.

MULDER
About the conspiracy?

WELL-MANICURED MAN
I think of it as an agreement. A word your father liked to use.

MULDER
I want to know where Scully is.
The Well-Manicured Man suddenly reaches into his jacket pocket, without warning or explanation. Mulder tensing slightly. He removes a thin felt envelope.

WELL-MANICURED MAN
The location of Agent Scully. And the means to save her life.
(off Mulder's look)
Please...
He gestures toward the car where the Driver stands with the back door open. Mulder hesitates, then steps from the doorway. Moving past the W. M. M., sliding in. The

W. M. M. gets in after him, closes the door. The car pulls away.

INT. LIMOUSINE - NIGHT - CONTINUOUS
WE SEE MULDER in the back seat, reflected in the rear-view mirror. Where we also see the eyes of the
DRIVER watching him. Mulder is handed the felt envelope by the W. M. M.

MULDER
What is it?

WELL-MANICURED MAN
A weak vaccine against the virus Agent
Scully has been infected with. It must be administered with ninety six hours.

MULDER
(beat)
You're lying.

WELL-MANICURED MAN
No. Though I have no way to prove otherwise. The virus is extraterrestrial. We know very little about it, except that it is the original inhabitant of this planet.

MULDER
(dubious, to say the least)
A virus?

WELL-MANICURED MAN
A simple, unstoppable lifeform. What is a virus but a colonizing force that cannot be defeated? Living in a cave, underground, until it mutates. And attacks.

MULDER
This is what you've been conspiring to conceal? A disease?

WELL-MANICURED MAN
No! For God sake you've got it all backwards.
This outburst comes suddenly, unexpectedly.

WELL-MANICURED MAN
Aids, the ebola virus -- on the evolutionary scale they are newborns.
This virus walked the planet long before the dinosaurs.

MULDER
What do you mean, walked?

WELL-MANICURED MAN
Your aliens, Agent Mulder, your little green men, first landed here millions of years ago. Those that didn't leave have been laying dormant underground since the last Ice Age. In the form of an evolved pathogen. Waiting to be reconstituted when the alien race from which it came returns to colonize the planet. Using us as hosts. Against this we have no defense. Nothing but a weak vaccine.
(beat)
Do you see why it was kept secret? Why even the best men -- men like your father -- could not let the truth be known?
The force and conviction of his delivery leave Mulder shaken.

WELL-MANICURED MAN
Until Dallas, we believed the virus was simply a controlling organism.
That mass infection would make us a slave race.

MULDER
That's why you bombed the building.
The infected firemen, the boy --

WELL-MANICURED MAN
Imagine our surprise when they began to gestate. My group has been working cooperatively with the alien colonists, facilitating their programs. To give us access to the virus. In false hope we might be able to secretly find a cure. So that we might save ourselves, as the last of the species.
(beat)
Your father wisely refused to believe this, choosing hope over selfishness.
Hope is the only future he had: his children,
(beat, then self-revealing)
The only future any of us have.
This draws a look back in the mirror from the Driver.

MULDER
But... he sacrificed his own daughter.
My sister, Samantha.

WELL-MANICURED MAN
The only true survivors of the viral holocaust will be those immune to it: those vaccinated against it and human/alien hybrids. Your father arranged for your sister's abduction.
He allowed her to be taken to an alien hybrid program, so that she would survive. As a clone.
(beat)
He had different hopes for you. That you would uncover the truth about the

Project. That you would stop it. That you would fight the future.
Mulder sits stunned by this. As if somehow his destiny has been validated, if not pre-ordained. Or maybe just justified.

MULDER
Why are you telling me this?

WELL-MANICURED MAN
I thought it only fair you should know, given how hard you've worked.

MULDER
What happened to Kurtzweil?

WELL-MANICURED MAN
As your father knew, things need to be sacrificed to the future.

MULDER
Where is he?

WELL-MANICURED MAN
Dr. Kurtzweil is in the trunk.
Mulder stares at the W. M. M. , at his cold-blooded expression.

MULDER
Let me out. Stop the car.

WELL-MANICURED MAN
(motioning)
Driver.
Mulder reaching to this as the limo pulls to a stop.
Trying the door, but the door is locked. When he turns back to the W. M. M. he has produced a handgun, which is now pointing at Mulder. Laid casually across a folded arm. Mulder reacts on seeing it.

WELL-MANICURED MAN
The men I work with will stop at nothing to clear the way for what they believe is their stake in the inevitable future. I was ordered to kill Kurtzweil. A necessary action to protect my grandchildren's lives.
(beat)
I might just as easily kill you.
Mulder is recoiling as he says this. Then, without hesitation in one quick move, he SHOOTS the Driver in the head.
The blood spattering on the front windshield -- and on

Mulder who has barely had a chance to react.

WELL-MANICURED MAN
Trust no one, Mr. Mulder.
Mulder looks at The Well-Manicured Man, expecting to be next. And for a moment, we do too. But the W. M. M. simply opens the door and steps out of the car. Holding the door open for Mulder who is still frozen by the actions that went just before.

EXT. DESOLATE D. C. STREET - NIGHT
Mulder steps out of the car, holding the felt envelope.
The Well-Manicured Man stands with a sober, intense look.

WELL-MANICURED MAN
(with quiet force)
You have precious little time. What
I've given you the alien colonists have no idea exists. You hold in your hand the power to end the project.

MULDER
How?

WELL-MANICURED MAN
The vaccine you hold is the only defense against the virus. Its introduction into an alien environment may have the power to destroy the delicate plans we've so assiduously protected for the last fifty years.
(beat)
Or it may not.

MULDER
What alien environment?

WELL-MANICURED MAN
Find Agent Scully. Save her. Only her science can save the future.

MULDER
What about you?

WELL-MANICURED MAN
My life is over.
(beat)
Go.
Mulder stands speechless for a moment. Until the W. M. M. points the weapon he's still holding at him.

WELL-MANICURED MAN
Go now!

And Mulder does. Moving away from the car, looking back over his shoulder. As the Well-Manicured Man gets back into the limousine, closes the door. A moment later...
THE CAR EXPLODES INTO FLAMES, knocking Mulder to the ground.

ANGLE ON MULDER
The felt envelope has been jarred from his grasp. Its contents loosed from inside: a piece of paper with
COORDINATES on it and an AMPULE and SYRINGE.
Mulder gets up, looks back. Then he picks up the envelope and its contents -- and begins to run. Running as fast as he can go. Until, far down the block, he disappears.
As the SCREEN DISSOLVES TO WHITENESS -- under which we hear an ominous low end Dolby THX Big Screen rumble. The same sound that opened our story.
Then there is movement, as the curvilinear line of a horizon becomes visible, bi-secting the screen between the white of the earth and the white of the sky. We are:

EXT. POLE OF INACCESSIBILITY - ANTARCTICA
Across the expanse of whiteness, a DARK IMAGE appears on the long flat horizon. Moving toward us. As a LEGEND appears, to establish.

CLOSER ON A SNOW TRACTOR
Crawling across the harsh frozen land like a domed insect.

INT. SNOW TRACTOR
Agent Mulder sits behind the controls of the enclosed cabin, several days growth on his face. Dressed in thick, bundled outerwear. He maneuvers the vehicle to a stop. Reaching for a handheld GPS monitor to check his position. Catching his breath for a moment -- all movement is exertion in this climate. Mulder stares hard out the front window, the wipers beating time, but there is nothing out there but whiteness. He wipes the fog from a side window with his gloved hand, seeing nothing but more whiteness. Checking the GPS device again, then reaching for the door latch.

RESUME WIDE EXTERIOR
Agent Mulder exits the vehicle, hopping down onto the snowscape crust. Setting out on foot with the GPS device held before him. In this forbidding environment he might as well be taking a space walk -- without the security of a lifeline. Which is the impression we get as his tiny figure trudges across the ice, increasing the distance between himself and the snow tractor.

MOVING WITH MULDER
Up a gentle grade, the snow tractor now behind him.

Moving into tight f. g. where he stops, seeing something now which allows him to pocket the GPS device. Dropping instinctively to his knees, so as to avoid being seen by:

MULDER'S POV
In the distance is an ICE STATION. A row of interconnecting WHITE DOME TENTS, whose design is now familiar to us. There are what look like snow tractors and other snow vehicles parked alongside the structures.

RESUME MULDER
Pulling a compact pair of binoculars from one of his deep jacket pockets. Training them on:

THE ICE STATION - BINO MATTE
PANNING across the domes and vehicles, where there is no sign of personnel -- until MULDER PANS off the building, finding in his field glasses AN APPROACHING SNOW
TRACTOR. Moving across the landscape toward the ice station. When it pulls to a stop, A MAN exits out of one of the domes: THE CIGARETTE SMOKING MAN. Moving to the vehicle and getting in.
The vehicle reverses now, transporting the CSM back away from the ice station.

CLOSE ON MULDER
Taking the field glasses away from his eyes. The excitement he feels expressed now in his breathing, which has become harder and shallower. Mulder rises, beginning to move the still great distance between himself and the ice station.

WIDE ON SCREEN
Mulder moving slowly across the white horizon toward the domed tents.

LOW ANGLE ON MULDER'S FEET
Moving cautiously, and with effort on the snowscape crust. CAMERA RISING up to Mulder's face, determined and watchful.

FOLLOWING MULDER
The ice station still several hundred yards in the distance, when MULDER SUDDENLY FALLS OUT OF FRAME, disappearing into a hole in the snowscape crust that just moments earlier had been stable footing.

HARD
INT. SNOW ICE BUBBLE - CONTINUOUS
Where Mulder's body falls through a ceiling of snowscape crust, landing on his back with a THUD on a hard surface. It takes him a moment to catch his breath, somewhat

reminiscent of Stevie at the beginning of the picture. Wincing through the pain. Until he turns over, regaining his wits, and his bearings.

NEW ANGLE
Mulder has fallen on a hard, narrow metallic structure.
Its dull black color a stark contrast to the white ice it's encased in. The bubble has been created by air coming out of vents in the structure, carving out corresponding patterns in the ceiling; softening the ice and snow above.

CLOSER ON MULDER
rising to his knees, the AIR from one of these vents blowing onto his face. Pulling off the hood of his jacket, looking deep into the vent which is open, ungrated.
And big enough for a man to crawl into. Which, after considering the hole he's fallen through high above him, is really Mulder's only choice.

INT. RIBBED CORRIDOR DUCT - CONTINUOUS
Mulder pulls himself forward through the ribbed corridor duct with his elbows, moving lizard-like into the constricted darkness.

INT. UPPER RIBBED CORRIDOR - CONTINUOUS
Above a frozen ice lith, Mulder's head appears, squeezing his shoulders and body out of a venting. With effort, Mulder slides out of the small space, using some architecture above as a handhold. Pulling his legs free and dropping onto the floor.

MULDER'S POV
It is dark in here, the features of the corridor ill-defined.

RESUME MULDER - WIDER
Mulder pulls a flashlight from a pocket in his parka, snicks it on. Its beam reflecting off tall frozen liths of ice regularly spaced on both sides of the corridor.

NEW ANGLE ON MULDER
Training the light down the corridor, which curves away in both directions. Then pointing it at something right in front of his nose: something that gives him a start.
Reaching up with his hand to brush away frost from the lith. Finding A MAN FROZEN IN ICE. Naked, his eyes staring into some long-forgotten distance. His hair is dark, his flat features familiar to us. He is the prehistoric hunter from the opening scenes of the movie.
His flesh has the opaque, see-through quality that we've seen before. Inside of which, frozen along with the man, is an EMBRYONIC CREATURE.

REVERSE ON MULDER
Reacting to this sight, then moving off down the corridor, his pace quickened.

EXT. POLE OF INACCESSIBILITY - ANTARCTICA
LOW ANGLE on the great white expanse. Across which a snow tractor is moving. PANNING with the vehicle to...
Mulder's snow tractor, where the first tractor stops, its headlights trained on Mulder's ride.
A beat, then the discovering machine moves out again, following the tracks that Mulder has left, which brings it STRAIGHT TOWARD CAMERA. As it passes us, we can see the DRIVER and the Cigarette Smoking Man sitting in the cabin. As we:

CUT BACK TO:
INT. UPPER RIBBED CORRIDOR - CONTINUOUS
MULDER comes to the end of the dim ice corridor where soft light is penetrating through several low, arched openings.
Mulder has to drop down to his knees to see into the openings.

ANGLE FROM OPPOSITE SIDE OF THE BALCONY PASSAGEWAY
Where Mulder is seen looking TOWARD CAMERA. The Balcony passageway is short. Mulder drops to his stomach again, pulling himself through, toward us. When he reaches the opposite end, Mulder pokes his head out, looking up in wonder at:

INT. CENTRAL THEATER - BALCONY - CONTINUOUS - WIDE ON
A STADIUM-SIZED DOME -- (CGI SET EXTENSION)
Imagine a domed sports arena -- this is the scope and scale of the space that Mulder has penetrated. We see him as only a small speck on a balcony midway between floor and ceiling. Pulling himself out of the balcony passageway, which is like countless other passageways.
Which are actually ventilation ports.

ANGLE OVER MULDER
Pulling himself to his feet. Beholding the space before him. Looking down to the center floor where a large central theater gives off a light different from elsewhere in the dome. An icy, bright glow. Leading down to the central theater far below are several LARGE TUBULAR SPOKES. (One of which leads up right next to
Mulder's position.)

ANGLE ON MULDER
Reacting to this. Then something captures his attention.

MULDER'S POV
There on the floor, far down below, is THE BUBBLE LITTER

Scully was transported in. (NOTE* Scully's clothes are still in the bubble litter.) Standing out as a rather human artifact against the otherwise dull gray bulwarks and architecture surrounding it.

INT. CENTRAL THEATER - BALCONY - CONTINUOUS - WIDE ON MULDER
looks beside him where the joint that connects two sections of one of the long tube spokes is designed with an allowance -- a separation that might allow a man to slip through the joint into the tube. Which is what
Mulder does here.

INT. TUBULAR SPOKE - CONTINUOUS
WIDE ANGLE FROM INSIDE TUBE TERMINUS
Mulder squeezing through into the tube, looking down past what looks like a chair lift-like track, on which the chairs are actually empty cryopod mechanisms; the same structures Mulder saw in the ribbed corridor in which bodies were encased in ice. Except these cryopods are empty.
Mulder begins to creep down TOWARD CAMERA, picking his way around the empty cryopods.

REVERSE ANGLE ON MULDER
Creeping away from us. Heading toward:

INT. LOWER CRYOPOD CORRIDOR
Where Mulder pops out at the lower tube terminus. Which leads into this bulwarked corridor at the base of the large stadium structure. Where:

REVERSE ON THIS CORRIDOR
Where Mulder is walking past frozen CRYOPODS hanging on a track. Each icy pod containing a HUMAN BODY frozen within. Partially visible behind clear blue ice. But these are modern men, and women. Their expressions a confused horror, as if they have been somehow frozen alive. They are slowly tracking.
Walking along the slowly moving carousel of frozen humanity. Stopping, turning, almost as if having sensed:

NEW ANGLE OVER OPPOSITE CRYOPOD
PUSHING IN ON MULDER'S FACE. Recording the horror and fear he's experiencing, on seeing:

CAMERA RISING UP A FROSTY WALL OF BLUE ICE
Where a woman's body is encased, its naked features hidden behind the opacity of the newly frozen blue crust. But whose face is unmistakable as that of Agent

Scully's. Frozen in a similar expression of far-away horror, her eyes cast slightly heavenward.

MULDER
hurries to get his jacket unzipped. Removing the FELT
ENVELOPE, removing the syringe body, the needle and the

AMPULE.
Hastily putting the syringe together, getting the needle poked into the soft rubber cap of the ampule. Bleeding the syringe now, the substance inside squirting out of the end of the needle onto the floor of the ship.
And the moment it does, the whole floor SIZZLES like water being dropped onto a hot skillet. Spreading out from Mulder in every direction. A VIOLENT CHEMICAL REACTION, as predicted by the man who gave him this substance. A moment later the entire structure Mulder is in SHUNTS. Shuddering violently and setting up a low-end RUMBLE. Causing Mulder to accidentally drop the syringe.

LOW CLOSE ANGLE
on the floor, where the syringe hits and bounces, but does not break or leak. Mulder scrambling into frame to re-collect it. Seeing the floor where the liquid from the syringe hit -- where it has been ETCHED AWAY by the substance.

EXT. HULL OF SPACESHIP/ICY BUBBLE - CONTINUOUS
Where Mulder crawled into the duct. Condensed air is streaming out of all the ducts now. The ice and snow above beginning to melt from the force and heat of the blasting all.

CUT BACK TO:
EXT. ICE STATION - CONTINUOUS
We can hear low end rumble and vibration. TWO DOZEN MEN are streaming out of the dome tents. Moving to their carious snow tractors and starting the vehicles.
A small exodus, the tractors pulling out of camp in a rush. Heading off in various directions.
CAMERA FINDING THE CIGARETTE SMOKING MAN moving to his tractor, with THE MAN WHO SHOT MULDER. Taking the last drag of his cigarette before throwing it into the snow.
He stares down at it a moment, as if caught in the grip of some emotion conflicting with duty.
The Man who shot Mulder inside the tractor now, throwing open the door for the CSM.

MAN WHO SHOT MULDER
C'mon. It's all going to hell.
He climbs up onto the vehicle, gets in and closes the door. And the vehicle pulls away as we:

CUT BACK TO:
INT. LOWER RIBBED CORRIDOR - CONTINUOUS - AGENT MULDER
Back on his feet, SMASHING now at the crust of brittle blue-ice that encases Scully. BASHING, SMASHING and then finally breaking through the hard outer later, its inner slushy contents spilling out of the puncture that exposes Scully's face and shoulder. Watery aqua-tinted liquid drains from her mouth and nose. But Scully is not conscious, and there is no indication she is even alive, her face frozen in a blank, almost beatific expression.

OVER MULDER TO SCULLY
As he plunges the needle into Scully's arm at the front of her shoulder. To which there is an immediate reaction
-- as if given a shot of adrenalin. Her eyes blinking away the cold moisture.

MULDER
Scully --
Scully's lips move goldfish-like as she tries to suck in air, an almost fearful expression overcoming her like a swimmer who's been held under too long. But no words are coming out yet.

MULDER
Breathe -- can you breathe?!
Scully is straining to do just that -- when liquid suddenly SPEWS from Scully's mouth. And she begins to cough and gag -- taking big gulps of air as her eyes focus on Mulder as if on a phantom, or a miracle.
Finally faint words ushering forth, whispering breaths that Mulder cannot discern.

MULDER
What?

CLOSE ON MULDER AND SCULLY
As he leans into her, putting his ear up to her mouth.
As the softest sound comes out in Scully's frosty breath.

SCULLY
Cold...

MULDER
Hang on. I'm going to get you out of here.
As she continues to suck air.

EXT. HULL OF SPACESHIP/ICE BUBBLE - CONTINUOUS

The hot air blasting from the ducts is causing the ice pack above to melt and collapse.

EXT. ICE STATION - CONTINUOUS - WIDE
As the ice tractors head away in all directions from the domed structures. A misty fog now emanating from the seams of the domes. Heat and condensation.

CUT BACK TO:
INT. UPPER RIBBED CORRIDORS - CONTINUOUS
Filling with misty condensation, too. The small beams of light that lighted Mulder's way earlier are now small shafts piercing the gathering interior cloud.
Illuminating:

THE PREHISTORIC MAN
Frozen in his icy pod, the hard semi-translucent surface of which is now etched with small streams of water running to the floor. Everything is melting and in motion.
Including the CREATURE which is vaguely visible inside the frozen man. It TURNS slightly inside the body, like an animal in utero. Its eyes now looking at us, blinking. As it presses against its own fleshy container, the body of its human host.

CUT BACK TO:
INT. LOWER RIBBED CORRIDOR - CONTINUOUS
It, too, is filling with misty condensation.

VARIOUS SHOTS
Of the ice encasing the human forms sweating and melting.
CAMERA ADJUSTING UP TO REVEAL Mulder pulling Scully along in a fireman's carry. She is dressed now in
Mulder's snow parka and the outer nylon pants he was wearing. Scully's legs are weak beneath her. Her body limp, but not lifeless. Mulder laboring to get her up the INTERIOR of the steep curving cylinder spoke, as the air fills with mist.

INT. LONG TUBE TERMINUS
NEW ANGLE ON MULDER AND SCULLY - LOOKING DOWN THE TUBE
Moving toward along the now-halted cryopod carrier hanging from the transport track. Mulder struggling against his own fading energy, pulling Scully up toward:

ANGLE ON BALCONY/CATWALK
Mulder pushing Scully up, though she seems to have at least some limited ability to do this on her own. The
DEEP, LOW RUMBLE we heard in the open frames of the movie reaching full volume now. The whole environment vibrating as Mulder boosts Scully up on the catwalk.
Climbing up over the prostrate body. Picking her up from the floor, pulling her back into the fireman's carry.

INT. LOWER RIBBED CORRIDOR - CONTINUOUS
Where the bodies are all beginning to melt.
VARIOUS SHOTS of rivulets of water forming on the icy liths that encase the bodies. The water from them seeping onto the circular central floor. The condensing mist thick and swirling.

CLOSE ON PODS
Where the body it houses seems to move. Though AS CAMERA
PUSHES IN we see that it is the creature inside this body moving, as if the heat and the defrosting are bringing the embryos to life.

INT. UPPER RIBBED CORRIDOR - CONTINUOUS - ANGLE DOWN CORRIDOR
Scully's head pokes through now, as she's pushed through the opening that Mulder used earlier to get into the vaulted arena. Pushed in fits and starts until she's all the way through. Mulder now straining and squeezing to do the same on his own.
The corridor is filled with heavy condensed mist now as
Mulder finally slips out of the low passageway, trying to get his bearing now as he huddles low over Scully.
Turning his attention to her as she COUGHS HOARSELY -- in some kind of acute spasm of pain -- but alive.

MULDER
We've got to keep moving.

SCULLY
(weakly)
Where are we?

MULDER
You got me. But I think I know what they did with Jimmy Hoffa.
Scully is struggling now as Mulder tries to pull her to her feet again. In real physical pain.

SCULLY
I can't...
Scully can't finish speaking, her voice becoming a hoarse cough.

SCULLY
(barely a whisper)
I can't go any farther.

MULDER

Yes you can. You're going to make it,
Scully.
Mulder hauling Scully up off the floor AWAY FROM CAMERA now.

NEW ANGLE ON RIBBED CORRIDOR
CAMERA MOVING THROUGH SPACE in the empty corridor, moving at a speed equal to Mulder and Scully's as they round the semi-circular ribbed corridor to meet us. Coming out of the mist, Scully back in the fireman's carry. Approaching the place where Mulder slipped down into the corridor.
Mulder stopping and seeing:

THE BODY IN THE MELTING ICE LITH
As it too moves, the embryonic creature inside it turning slightly, as if coming awake.

REVERSE ON MULDER
Reacting to this -- and then to Scully who suddenly starts GASPING FOR BREATH. Falling now from Mulder's grasps as her legs buckle and she goes down.

LOW ANGLE ON SCULLY
Her face is going red, straining for air. Her eyes rolling, seeking relief. As Mulder drops down beside her.

MULDER
Shit --
But she is unable to answer. Mulder hastening to unzip her/his jacket. To get to her neck and find a pulse.

MULDER
Scully --
Mulder cannot find a pulse. Scully straining harder now as Mulder reaches his fingers into her mouth, clearing her passageway. Moving on top of her now, and pumping forcefully on her chest -- trying to get air into her.
One - two - three.
And putting his mouth down to hers (FINALLY!), breathing his life into her. Pulling away from her to see that he is unsuccessful at this -- that Scully is continuing to strain. Pumping her chest again --

MULDER
You're not dying on me now -- godammit godammit godammit --
As he pumps her chest. Placing his mouth over hers again and BREATH - BREATH -- BREATH.
Lifting his mouth from hers, feeling for a pulse again, putting his eat down to her mouth, praying he'll feel the breeze of a breath. Nothing. While:

ANGLE OVER HIM TO THE CREATURE IN THE ICY POD
As it moves again, MORE VIOLENTLY NOW. As the ice around it continues to melt and fissure.

RESUME MULDER
His hands going to a pocket on the inside of the jacket
Scully is wearing -- his jacket -- finding again the syringe that he used on Scully. It is still partially full of vaccine. Mulder finding this, getting ready to use it when --
-- Scully's body suddenly comes back to life beneath him. Labored breaths which turn into a coughing spasm.
Mulder breaths relievedly for a moment, watching Scully coughing, coming back to life. Her eyes trying to focus on him, finding him. Seeing his labored relief. The panic melting away.

SCULLY
(weakly, pained whisper)
Mulder...
She wants to tell him something. He leans down next to her.

SCULLY
(continued weak)
Had you big time.
Mulder has but a moment to savor this weary victory though when he REACTS to something, that causes him to

WHIP HIS HEAD AROUND.
MULDER'S POV DOWN RIBBED CORRIDOR
Through the condensed mist he can see CREATURES
BEGINNING TO HATCH, sprouting from the melted ice-encased bodies they have gestated in. Their THREE
FINGERED HANDS beating at the soft ice. Their powerful feet kicking at it, too.

RESUME MULDER
Looking the other way down the corridor, seeing --

MORE CREATURES
The slushy material that makes up the inner core spilling out with them as the creatures KICK out of their tombs.

RESUME MULDER
Lifting Scully up with all his strength he has left in him. He's got to get her overhead now, back up the venting that he slipped down from. She is weak and of little help.

Mulder gets her propped up on his strength so that he can use the power of his legs to boost her toward the opening. Which puts him face to face with THE EMBRYONIC CREATURE. Its eye looking directly at him, blinking, before it goes into another FITFUL SPASM inside its host body.

ANGLE DOWN FROM VENT
Where Scully is boosted up TOWARD CAMERA. Her hands reaching feebly for something to grab onto. Finding a handhold.

MULDER
Keep breathing, Scully.
She utters something guttural, unintelligible as the next thrust up from Mulder gets her head and shoulders into the opening of the vent.

RESUME MULDER
Beneath her, pushing with all his might. His hands under her shoes now, forcing her up into the vent like a rolled carpet into the rafters.

RESUME SCULLY
Struggling with her arms and elbows, barely conscious, but somehow able to manage herself forward.

RESUME MULDER
Pushing Scully up the last little way. Then reaching up to find a handhold for himself. Grabbing hold and lifting himself as one of his feet kicks at the ice -- where the creature he was just face to face with BURSTS from its icy pod. One hand, then the other shooting out of the ice where they have broken through the host.
Ripping open the front of the body, including the man's face. Making a slimy, gaping tear in what was formerly flesh.
Its hands grabbing at Mulder as he thrashes to free himself from it getting a grip.
As Mulder struggles to pull himself up, fighting off the creature which he cannot see beneath him.

RESUME CREATURE
As it emerges from the ice, still grasping and TEARING at Mulder's legs with its claws. But as it BURSTS
COMPLETELY from its place, Mulder is able to pull himself up and into the vent in one athletic movement.

ANGLE FROM INSIDE THE VENT - SCULLY
lies motionless in the ducting, her body forced forward by Mulder's in this last surging move.

TIGHT ANGLE ON MULDER
Drawing his legs up quickly inside. Not wasting a moment shoving Scully's butt forward in front of him.

MULDER
Scully -- you breathing?

RESUME SCULLY
Letting out another low, guttural sound -- which STRAINS out of her with each push forward.

EXT. SNOW/ICE BUBBLE - CONTINUOUS
Scully's head and arms push up through the vent where
Mulder first entered. The ice and snow surrounding it, which had created the bubble structure, have melted and fallen. So that above Scully's larger hole has opened up to the surface. The air is full of condensation, swirling around them.

ANGLE FROM ABOVE - THROUGH THE HOLE IN THE ICE
Where, through the swirling steam we see Mulder push
Scully clear of the vent. Climbing free himself now.
When the surface they are upon SHUDDERS AND QUAKES. As if it has come unloosed, destabilized.
And with this comes A MIGHTY FORCE OF STEAM from the vent Mulder and Scully just crawled from. Blasting up past them with terrible HISSING FORCE. Causing Mulder to throw Scully away from its superheated energy.
Pulling her up the now climbable embankment created by the melting snow; pulling her toward the surface of the ice sheet.

EXT. POLE OF INACCESSIBILITY - ANTARCTICA - WIDE
Where a wide radius of steam rises from similar and regularly spaced holes in the ice sheet, defining a circular structure beneath. The White Domed Tents of the ice station are in the center of this, dwarfed by the enormity of the melting radius.

RESUME MULDER AND SCULLY
Mulder pulling her up the softened and collapsed snow.
The hot steam blasting up with hideous force behind them. The sound DEAFENING.

NEW ANGLE OVER MULDER AND SCULLY
Pulling her to the surface of the ice sheet where behind them in the distance the ICE STATION can be seen through the atmosphere of condensed air. When suddenly the ice beneath it gives way and the ice station falls away, caving in to the center of the radius. Which is what begins to happen to the rest of the ice sheet that spreads out to where Mulder and Scully are standing.

Causing Mulder to realize:

MULDER
(over the din)
We've got to run!

She is weak, but is able to find her footing. Dragged behind Mulder as the ice behind them begins to break away, falling down into an ever-expanding center and sending up magnificent geysers of steam created by the superheated surface below.

WIDE ON SCENE
Mulder and Scully running AT CAMERA just ahead of the collapsing center. The mass of ice around them beginning to break up. Steam vents erupting instantaneously everywhere.

HIGH ANGLE ON SCENE
A black dome is becoming visible through the giant circle of steam, in the ever-widening center hole that
Mulder and Scully are running from. Which is chasing them to the edge of the radius.

ANGLE FOLLOWING MULDER AND SCULLY
As Mulder struggles to pull Scully fast enough to outrace the icy debris that is tumbling away just behind them. Large chunks falling and bouncing off the superheated surface below, blown back up like water being dropped onto a hot skillet.

EXTREMELY HIGH AND WIDE
The Agents mere specks fleeing the circle of churning ice and steam. As it cascades away in three hundred and sixty degrees. From here the deafening sound if absorbed into the vastness, tricking us of the reality of the massive movement of frozen material down below.

ANGLE LEADING MULDER AND SCULLY
As Scully loses her footing, falling to the ground.
Mulder dragging her back up to her feet, though, maintaining forward momentum. While behind them the thundering force of the superheated melting snow and ice is moving in on them.
And then suddenly -- MULDER AND SCULLY are gone!
The radial edge of the falling snow continuing only a few feet beyond where they disappeared. The violent upheaval of snow abating but slightly. Beat, beat...
THEN THE AGENTS APPEAR AGAIN. Thrust upward by a RISING
BLACK PRECIPICE which catapults them off its leading edge. As they fall the distance to the sheet of ice below.

LOW ANGLE ON ICE SHEET

Where the Agents hit hard on the ice sheet. The rain of ice chunks pounding all around them. As the monolithic wall of the craft continues to rise.
Mulder trying to get to Scully in this hail of debris which he shields his face from.

WIDE ON LEADING EDGE
Rising faster now out of the earth as it begins to increasingly shed and break free of the frozen weight it carried. Until the bottom of the edge of the wall appears, lifting clear of the ice sheet and the crater that held it.

EXTREME HIGH WIDE ANGLE ON SPACE SHIP
Where now we see the scope and shape of the ship, which is breathtaking. The domed center sloping off to a gentle gradient, which is the surface that Mulder and
Scully were running on. The ship is now slowly rotating as it moves upward in a gently rising hover.
Mulder and Scully are on the ice sheet below.

RESUME MULDER AND SCULLY
Scully face down on the ice. Mulder lifting his head when THE HEAVY SHADOW of the ship comes over them.
Looking up from this position to see:

THE SPACE SHIP
Moving slowly, laterally just overhead. Thunderously rumbling. The dark detail of its underside visible in this angle. As it continues to rise, the shadow passing over Mulder and Scully.

NEW ANGLE OVER MULDER AND SCULLY
Scully is still face down on the ice, as Mulder watches the ship's shadow cast over Mulder's SnowCat which is still parked in the distance. Moving up and off.
The ship continues up into the Antarctic sky where it rises toward the sky where it begins to get WHITEHOT.
Transforming itself into pure energy. It is visible for several moments during transformation. Then it disappears completely. As it does the RUMBLE, which dopplers across the white, barren landscape. Then it is gone.

MULDER
Watches this then lays his head down on Scully's back.
He is spent, at the brink of complete exhaustion. His whole body heaving. But now starting to shiver, and to lose consciousness.
Scully's body is motionless beneath him, for a moment we might believe that this is the way it might end. Out here on the ice with Mulder and Scully freezing to death. A chill wind blows off the Antarctic plain, the same LOW RUMBLE, the only taint of silence in vastness of this literal end of the world.

Then Scully coughs -- the same hoarse cough. She's alive. Struggling to consciousness. Her head lifting slightly, TURNING TO CAMERA. Her eyes blink open and she coughs again. Feeling Mulder's weight on top of her, unaware of his condition or even where she is.

SCULLY
(weakly)
Mulder...

There is no answer. Scully struggling to pull herself out from under the weight of his body. Rolling over so that her face is opposite Mulder's now. Seeing that he has lost consciousness. Finding the strength to roll him over, so that she can cradle him and warm him.

HIGH WIDE ANGLE ON THIS SCENE
With the Snowcat a short distance away, Mulder and
Scully in each others arms. The way it should end.

FADE TO BLACK
Silence. Longer than we would like. Long enough to make us nervous, then certain, then angry. Then... we FADE UP a prelap of the sound of a CRACKLING FIRE.

FADING UP ON:
EXT. ACRES OF CORN - MAGIC HOUR
TRACKING LOW WITH MEN IN FATIGUES, moving along the perimeter of the corn field as they set fire to the corn stalks with small handheld butane burners. While other Men in Fatigues are moving between the rows dousing the furrows with accelerant.

DISSOLVE TO:
INT. FBI FIELD OFFICE - DALLAS - NIGHT
The large room filled with the evidence and debris from the bombing. It is dark. Until A FLASHLIGHT BEAM pricks the blackness, moving toward us into f. g. Carried by the man we now recognize as The Man Who Shot Mulder. He moves with directness, purpose. Finding what he's looking for amid the cataloged material, he finds on a work bench. Next to the microscope Scully had used. It is the BONE FRAGMENTS, held in an evidence container.
He pockets them and exits as quiet and directly as he entered.

DISSOLVE TO:
EXT. ACRES OF CORN - WIDE - CGI PLATE
The sky aglow with orange flames as the crops burn to the ground. We hold on this shot, PRELAPPING the sound of:

JANA CASSIDY'S VOICE

... in light of the report I've got before me; in light of the narrative I'm now hearing...

INT. FBI OFFICE OF PROFESSIONAL REVIEW - DAY
Jana Cassidy sits at the head of the desk, just as when we first met her.
She is flanked by the other members of the review board, including A. D. Skinner who sits at the end of the table.
Cassidy flips through a file she's referred to before she continues. Looking up with consternation as she resumes.

CASSIDY
... my official report is incomplete pending these new facts I'm being asked to reconcile. Agent Scully...

AGENT SCULLY
Sitting where she last sat, at the small table. The seat next to her conspicuously empty. Her face bears the signs of slight frostbite, somewhat healed. Her expression is even, her attitude composed, but her eyes are filled of dark, restrained defiance.

CASSIDY
... while there is direct evidence now that a federal agent may have been involved in the bombing... the other events you've laid down here seem too incredible on their own, and quite frankly implausible in their connection.
PANNING THE OTHER BOARD MEMBERS - curious, bemused like
Cassidy. Skinner shifts uncomfortably.

SCULLY
What is it you find incredible?

CASSIDY
Well... where would you like me to start? Antarctica is a long way from
Dallas, Agent Scully. I can't very well submit a report to the Attorney
General that alleges the links you've made here. Bees and corn crops do not quite fall under the rubric of domestic terrorism.

SCULLY
No, they don't.

CASSIDY
Most of what I find in here is lacking a coherent picture of an organization with an attributable motive. I realize you're very lucky to be alive Agent
Scully. The ordeal you've endured has clearly affected you -- though the holes in your account leave this panel with little choice but to delete these references from our final

report to the Justice Department. Until which time hard evidence becomes available that would give us cause to pursue such an investigation.
Scully has her hand in her coat pocket now. Moving around the table and approaching Cassidy. Removing something which she puts on the desk in front of her. A small vial.

SCULLY
I don't believe the FBI currently has an investigation unit qualified to pursue the evidence in hand.
Cassidy picks up the vial, studying the contents of this vial: the dead bee that stung Scully. Studying it as
Scully turns and moves to the door, without permission, no further adieu.

ANGLE TO INCLUDE A. D. SKINNER
Watching Scully exit.

CASSIDY (O. S.)
Mr. Skinner... . ?
CAMERA PIVOTING TO INCLUDE CASSIDY. Looking at him.

CASSIDY
Please ask Agent Scully to come back to this hearing. We're not quite finished.
As Skinner rises, unsure of the intent behind this directive, we:

DISSOLVE TO:
EXT. WASHINGTON D. C. - DAY
We are JUST ABOVE THE TREETOPS. The Capitol Dome is in the far distance. CAMERA CRANING DOWN to find Mulder sitting by himself on a park bench. We are WIDE. There is no one else around.
Until the Cigarette Smoking Man appears. Walking through the otherwise deserted park. Joining Mulder on the park bench.

CLOSER ON MULDER, THE CIGARETTE SMOKING MAN
They do not speak for several moments. A quite tension as the CSM lights up a trademark smoke. Inhaling, exhaling. Then:

CIGARETTE SMOKING MAN
Congratulations on your survival. Your life is worthless now, I hope you know that.

MULDER
And yours?

CIGARETTE SMOKING MAN
(derisive)

You think you've stopped it. What I've worked for fifty years to create. You haven't stopped it. You can't stop it.
(takes a drag)
You're just one man.

MULDER
You're wrong.

WIDE ANGLE
Mulder rises from the bench heading TOWARD CAMERA. The
CSM rising, watching him.
As Mulder continues toward us. ADJUST TO REVEAL Agent
Scully in the f. g. Mulder moving to her as the CSM watches from the distance. Their eyes meet, an unspoken restored bond exchanged in this moment. Before Mulder takes Scully by the arm, leads her off. Leaving the CSM standing alone in the distance. As we:

DISSOLVE TO:
EXT. CORN FIELDS/WHITE DOMES - TUNISIA - DAY
TRACKING LOW WITH A PAIR OF FEET
The wearer of them sporting peasant sandals. We realize shortly that while the feet are moving across sandy ground, that the foliage in the near b. g. is corn. And that the person we are tracking with is passing row after row of stalks.

CAMERA RISING AS IT TRACKS
REVEALING A TUNISIAN MAN dressed in peasant clothes. He is carrying a piece of paper. Moving with hasty purpose.
Stopping at the end of one of the long rows of corn where CONRAD STRUGHOLD is coming toward him. Making his way between rows of stalks. The Peasant waits patiently as Strughold approaches, handing him the piece of paper.
Strughold reads it, his otherwise steely countenance reflecting a disturbance seen only in the slight narrowing of his eyes.
He looks up at the Peasant and says something to him in
Tunisian Arabic. Said as command, which causes the
Peasant to nod dutifully and move off as he came.
Strughold stands for a moment, then crumples the paper slightly and drops it. Moving off down the same corn row in which he approached.
CAMERA DROPPING TO THE GROUND where we find the paper on which we see a flat section that is not so crumpled we cannot read the words: X-FILES RE-OPENED. STOP. PLEASE

ADVISE. STOP.

CAMERA RISING NOW. Rising up past the stalks. Where we can still see Strughold walking. RISING UP AND UP to reveal ACRES AND ACRES OF CORN. Many times more than we had seen previously. Stretched out across the Tunisian
Desert, ending only where THREE WHITE DOMES stand on the distant horizon. Off this image we FADE OUT.

THE END

Printed in Great Britain
by Amazon